The New Urba

The New Urban Question

Andy Merrifield

First published 2014 by Pluto Press
345 Archway Road, London N6 5AA

www.plutobooks.com

Distributed in the United States of America exclusively by
Palgrave Macmillan, a division of St. Martin's Press LLC,
175 Fifth Avenue, New York, NY 10010

British Library Cataloguing in Publication Data
A catalogue record for this book is available from the British Library

ISBN 978 0 7453 3484 4 Hardback
ISBN 978 0 7453 3483 7 Paperback
ISBN 978 1 7837 1135 2 PDF eBook
ISBN 978 1 7837 1137 6 Kindle eBook
ISBN 978 1 7837 1136 9 EPUB eBook

Library of Congress Cataloging in Publication Data applied for

This book is printed on paper suitable for recycling and made from fully
managed and sustained forest sources. Logging, pulping and manufacturing
processes are expected to conform to the environmental standards of the
country of origin.

10 9 8 7 6 5 4 3 2 1

Typeset from disk by Stanford DTP Services, Northampton, England
Text design by Melanie Patrick
Simultaneously printed digitally by CPI Antony Rowe, Chippenham, UK
and Edwards Bros in the United States of America

In Memory of
Marshall Berman (1940–2013),
friend and inspiration

Contents

Preface: Neo-Haussmannization and its Discontents

One of the defining features of democracy in modern times is its lack of democracy. Representative political institutions are meant to serve people, but end up serving themselves, as well as the economic interests that serve those in power; financial institutions are meant to enable peoples' economic capacity, yet end up screwing ordinary people, encumbering ordinary people with massive debts, ripping us off not only through malpractice and cheating (widespread as that is), but also through the normal everyday functioning of those institutions. For a long while people almost everywhere know that modern "democracy" is riddled with huge and incorrigible lies. But they frequently grin and bear those lies, come what may, both as individuals and families, inventing their own truths along the way, their own coping mechanisms, putting their heads down and getting on with life as best they can. Occasionally, very occasionally, people feel that democratic *lack* weighing too heavily and decide to do something about it, collectively. They take to the streets and organize themselves into a social movement, into a political movement that struggles for real democracy, even if those struggling have little idea of what "real" democracy might look like.

Over the past few years, people across the world have taken to the streets en masse, protesting against undemocratic political institutions and their leaders, and against undemocratic financial institutions and their bosses. They've done so—continue to do so—in the streets of hundreds of cities across the globe. In countries like Tunisia and Egypt, these democratic struggles have borne the label "Arab Spring," resembling the euphoric "Prague Spring" reform movement of 1968, when a seemingly intractable political structure was likewise brushed aside by the collective power of people yearning for something else. In Western countries, dissenting vocabularies still sound new and fresh yet have already become common parlance: Occupy, *Indignados*, the 99%, the New Majority, etc. What these groups all have in common, and what bonds their activism, is a popular dissatisfaction with current political-economic life, with a regime of capital accumulation that is *parasitic* through and through, that dispossesses. Parasites in government and parasites in business everywhere reinforce one another like a contagion, and feed off the larger "host" organism, chomping away at the common-wealth the world over, eating away inside the social body, squandering generative capacity by thriving exclusively off unproductive activities.

What equally unites these movements is how they've used prominent spaces of the city and new social media to express common grievance and collective solidarity. They've affirmed new forms of resistance, contesting, amongst other things, our hyper-exploitative undemocratic system of global governance as well as our hyper-exploitative undemocratic system of global urbanism—a dual, interrelated theme that this book intends to put under close scrutiny. Indeed, one of its chief concerns is to develop concepts that can *periodize* this system theoretically, while challenging this system politically, helping consolidate and advance ongoing activism and militancy, offering a theory that dialogues with politics, as well as a politics that dialogues with theory. Here concepts and activism mutually reinforce one another—or at least try to.

Theory and politics are thus central planks of *The New Urban Question*. At times, like in the opening chapter "Whither Urban Studies?," theory is approached from inside academia, done with the desire to open up academia, to get the sub-discipline of urban studies out into the world, beyond the specialist, beyond the positivist, beyond debates which see an ontological distinction between the "real world" and the world of scholarly theory, between knowledge and ideology, objectivity and subjectivity. For me, empiricism and positivism cripple our ability to understand more fully the major component of this "new" urban question: *neo-Haussmannization*. The incessant media hype and "expert" yapping about exploding urban populations, about the fact that *x* many people will be living in urban settlements in *y* number of years and that the percentage of urban dwellers will soon be reaching epic global proportions—all this Malthusian fear-mongering—obfuscates the class and power question surrounding our current urban question.

Neo-Haussmannization signifies a new riff on an old tale of urban redevelopment, of divide and rule through urban change, of altering and upscaling the urban physical environment to alter the social and political environment. What happened to mid-nineteenth-century Paris is now happening globally, not only in big capital cities and orchestrated by powerful city and national political-economic forces, but in all cities, orchestrated by transnational financial and corporate elites everywhere, endorsed by their respective national governments. While these class forces in and out of government aren't always consciously conspiring, they nonetheless create a global orthodoxy, one that's both creating and tearing apart a new urban fabric, one that clothes the whole wide world.

"Urban fabric" is a term I prefer to that of "cities." One reason is that this fabric stretches to envelop everywhere, irrespective of whether we see it physically embodied in bricks and mortar, in steel and concrete, in stuff we tend to normally associate with the constitution of cities. The "urban" is a more abstract and more concrete way to figure out the urbanization of the world, because it helps us think about a process that manifests itself in undergrowth as well as overgrowth, in abandonment as well as overcrowding, in underdevelopment as well as overdevelopment. The two flanks are intimately related, are part and parcel of the same life-form, the same life-force of active creation and creative destruction. If we delve into the nature of this fabric—as its thread woofs and warps the globe, from West to East, from East to West, from San Francisco to Vladivostok, from Shanghai to San Diego, as well as up and down between poles—if we probe this fabric like a quantum scientist might probe the subatomic universe, we find a strange micro-reality that is in fact a gigantic macro-reality.

Within this urban fabric old distinctions between the global North and global South, between inner city and suburb, between city and countryside are redundant, chaotic conceptions, requiring an upgrade and a rethink. Not least because inside the urban fabric today we see centers and peripheries all over the place, cities and suburbs within cities and suburbs, centers that are geographically peripheral, peripheries that suddenly become new centers. Meanwhile, the countryside finds itself urbanized and deindustrialized cities ruralize, actually witness nature fighting back. So it goes, in a world that knows no real borders yet seems everywhere to build walls. Planetary urbanization, as such, both unites and divides the world, unites and divides its planetary citizens.

In the old urban question, certainly as one of its proponents Manuel Castells conceived it in the 1970s, "the urban" found its definition relative to socialized goods and services, relative to "public" goods and services funded by the state; Castells labeled them items of "collective consumption," goods consumed in common, consumed collectively, like housing and schools, like hospitals and mass transit.[1] They're socialized goods functionally important in the reproduction of labor-power, he said: they ensure workers are housed, get to work on time, are educated by institutions whose ultimate *raison d'être* is to produce literate but compliant people, those who kowtow without too much fuss to the dominant order. Castells believed the urban question became a question of how the state managed this state of affairs, how it orchestrated collective consumption, how it planned and funded collective consumption, kept its own political legitimacy with its constituency over collective consumption. The urban, for Castells, was a "spatial unit" of this social reproduction, of the reproduction of labor-power; it wasn't defined as a spatial unit of production, because production, Castells said, operated regionally and increasingly globally. As for urban politics, from the Castellian standpoint two strands emerged: interventions by the state and interventions by ordinary people in the state's intervention. The state thereby mediated class and social struggle, diffused and deflected it, displaced and absorbed it, insofar as it intervened between capital and labor within the urban context.

Much of what follows in *The New Urban Question* highlights how Castells's urban question is now an archaic urban question: the stakes and arena of struggle have changed markedly since his day. To a large

1. Manuel Castells, *The Urban Question: A Marxist Approach*, Edward Arnold, London, 1977.

extent, Castells knew it himself; and this became one reason—an erroneous reason—why he felt he needed not only to abandon his old urban question (and *The Urban Question*), but also Marxism to boot. The Marxist baby went with the urban bathwater. For Castells, the whole motivation of urban politics was how ordinary people organized themselves into movements that assumed a different role to trade unions, expressed different agendas to official political parties, raised issues of neighborhood resources and urban self-management, working-class concerns about affordable housing, stuff outside the domain of traditional left organizations. Demands were often single-issue grievances, cutting across "formal" classes lines, involving petty-bourgeois, middle-class elements. In the mix, Castells identified a new political subject: *urban social movements*. As the 1970s unfolded and gave way to the 1980s, urban social movements sprang up in continental Europe—as elsewhere—contesting the state and demanding continued investment in collective consumption, continued investment in working people.

Fiscal crises and economic downturn scarred this era. A subsequent change of ideological and economic persuasion ensued, a change in how the capitalist state went about its business. Quite literally went about its business. This era, we know with hindsight, became an interregnum that would soon spawn neoliberalism. Castells's thesis began to crumble in the face of the inexplicable: collective consumption items, so vital for social reproduction, so functional for capital, so necessary for the overall survival of capitalism—how could it possibly be that the state would desist from funding them? And so it passed that rather than ideologically and materially sponsor people, the state began to ideologically and materially sponsor capital, especially financial and merchant capital, and a whole new urban question posed itself. The biggest drawback of Castells's old urban question is his passive rendering of the urban, that the urban is a spatial unit of reproduction rather than a space which capital *productively* plunders: capital now *actively* dispossesses collective consumption budgets and upscales land by valorizing urban space as a commodity, as a pure financial asset, exploiting it as well as displacing people. This is precisely where neo-Haussmannization raises its ugly political-economic head.

Pointing the theoretical finger at neo-Haussmannization, theorizing it with political intent, with militant intent, begets the other key aspect of *The New Urban Question*: what of urban politics? Immanent within neo-Haussmannization, as a global strategy, as a ruling-class strategy plundering and reorganizing the world, is not only *their* political necessity from above, but also *our* still-emergent immanent undertow from below. Neo-Haussmannization, in short, produces its Other, powers a dialectic of dispossession *and* insurrection, an accumulation strategy as well as a rebellion waiting and plotting in the wings. Hence its discontents. And this across the whole surface of the globe. Thus neo-Haussmanization is a process that can only be kept in check through a politics of space, through a para-militarization of space from above—sometimes literally above—using high-tech securization and surveillance. Rebellion from below, in the street, is invariably low-tech and slingshot; and, as such, the drama of neo-Haussmannization unfolds as a veritable urban civil war, expressing itself on both sides of the urban divide, in powerful centers as well as in marginalized peripheries, in the "global North" as well as the "global South," inside the outside as well as outside the inside; it is a war of walls and ramparts, of bankers and *banlieues*.

Still, it's difficult to know what is the precise *specificity* of urban social movements, if indeed there is any specificity? One might wonder what is it that "the urban" brings to the notion of "social movement"? These days, I'm more inclined to think that it's the idea of a social movement which defines the urban. In the past, in the "old" urban question, scholars like Castells looked toward the urban to resolve the problem of building a social movement. Now, we need to build a social movement to resolve the problem of the urban. Yet even here the idea of "social" sounds redundant and tautological. Won't all progressive mobilizations be somehow social? What needs affirming instead is more the creation of a *political movement*, one struggling to impose its singularity as a mass democratic movement, one that builds democracy through the scattered shards of social movements the world over. Such a democratic political movement implies that all disparate social movements, those struggling for local concerns (concerns that are now, willy-nilly, common global concerns), need to make themselves more important than they actually are; they need to publicize their activism, publicize their agendas and grievances to wider audiences, through alternative media, sharing tales of neoliberal crimes and misdemeanors and propelling themselves outwards, onto a planetary plane.

Like a lot of people, I've been inspired by the democracy struggles that have erupted around the world during the past few years, from the "Arab Spring" to activism that has been filed under the rubric "Occupy movement," the latest of which fills Istanbul's Taksim Square with bodies contesting Erdoğan's unyielding, top-down authoritarianism. Like Zuccotti Park and Tahrir Square, like Puerta del Sol and Syntagma Square, encounters between dissatisfied people in Taksim Square create a democratic moment at the bottom of society, while heralding a crisis of legitimacy at the top. And here again, asking to what extent these movements are urban seems to me the wrong question. A better one is: how do these movements redefine the notion of anti-capitalist politics, its present and future potentiality?

The political perils and possibilities of this democratic impulse are accorded considerable attention in *The New Urban Question*, even if I see no direct correlation between "good" theory and "efficacious" politics; the former doesn't necessarily lead to the latter. But theoretical explication—a deeper insight into what's happening to our urban world, how it is used as an accumulation strategy by wealthy, powerful people, how they produce spatial and social inequalities—all this might equip people with a capacity to think; to think through what we're up against, to channel one's anger and rage of *knowing*. Theory can highlight the generality of this process. (Hegel, remember, said thinking should form "intuitions of the whole.") Theory can teach us that we are in it all together, that resistance must be mass resistance, that this is the only way we can truly overcome the present.

Not too long ago, the late Stéphane Hessel invoked the need to "*Indignez-vous*," to get *outraged*.[2] We should be outraged, Hessel said, by the flouting of people's rights, by the ineptitude and unwillingness of governments everywhere to stand up for the rights of its citizens. Governments seem more concerned with subsidizing its financiers

2. Stéphane Hessel, *Indignez-vous!*, Indigène Éditions, Montpellier, 2011.

and free marketeers; or else have financiers and free marketeers become the government. It's high time, said Hessel, for citizens to stand up for themselves, time for mass indignation; it's time to affirm one's right to stand up for one's right. Hessel particularly wanted to incite young people whose future isn't entirely rosy under the current order; he wants 20-somethings to reject the *now*, to plot and hatch a peaceful insurrection.

The idea of insurrection has a long legacy in continental Europe. ("Rebellion" is perhaps its Anglo-Saxon equivalent, and there, too, there's a longish tradition.) "Insurrection" got its real inauguration in 1789 during the French Revolution; later it became a militant watchword in the worker and citizen struggles erupting throughout the 1840s, reaching its *dénouement* as well as its epochal limits in 1871, during the Paris Commune. In what follows, I want to look at some of these past struggles, struggles designed to rid ordinary people of both a parasitic aristocratic elite who exploited them, and a liberal bourgeois class who replaced this elite. These past struggles still speak in loud and resonant decibels. They can still educate us today; although these days insurrection—or Rebellion, upper-case "R"—cannot remain pacifist: violence inevitably enters the fray where dispossessed people see their rights flagrantly trampled on.

"Rights-talk," though, has never turned me on very much, and in this book I will say why. Human rights and other rights such as "right to the city" are much too important, much too pressing, to be left to hollow and abstract debates about rights alone. There are no bedrock universal rights that humans can invoke to defend themselves against injustice and oppression. At its broadest, there are two routes to resistance, two routes for gaining one's "rights"; and each case involves taking rather than asking; each case involves the law, on the one hand, and breaking of the law, on the other. In the latter sense, "violence" is ascribed by the law-keeper to the law-breaker, in much the same way that Margaret Thatcher always saw Nelson Mandela's African National Congress (ANC) as a violent, unlawful "terrorist" organization.

To uphold one's rights concretely means, then, to engage with the law, to get a gifted lawyer to interpret the letter of the law, to do so in a creative and progressive manner; to have him or her use the law not as a singularity but as a form of jurisprudence, as a philosophy of law—what *should* the law be?—as a law that takes a stand, that isn't neutral, that understands the link between "facts" and "values," between the legal system and moral justification (see Chapter 9). As critical legal scholars like Roberto Unger are wont to say, the law is slippery, contradictory and indeterminate and, accordingly, "full of transformative possibility." That said, assaulting and infiltrating ruling-class power institutions, like its judiciary, like its system of law and order, means both a stretching and a *breaking* of the law. Rebellion necessitates something unlawful in the eyes of rulers, something that transgresses their public order and civic code. In lots of instances, established laws are, in Plato's Thrasymachus's blunt terms (cf. *The Republic* Book I), written by *and for* the powerful; justice, in other words, is merely "what is advantageous to the stronger," what benefits the stronger and what is then enshrined as the accepted wisdom of the courts. Rebellion, conversely, utters the collective language that these laws are *wrong*, that we do not abide by them, that we will smash or amend these laws through organized, collective political engagement. It is the latter, law-breaking politics that interests me most in *The New Urban Question*, breaking bourgeois law to affirm popular democratic desire.

Either way, whether invoking or breaking the law, whether doing it inside or outside the courtroom, "rights-talk" never really enters the conversation. Both necessitate *pragmatism*: a pragmatism of the law and a pragmatism of Rebellion. There is no "right to the city" written in any constitution, other than a loosely defined dwelling and well-being right consecrated in the 1948 United Nations' Declaration of Human Rights. But here, especially, the indeterminacy of the language would leave even the most progressive and gifted lawyer yearning for an out-of-court settlement, for a settlement on the street. "Everyone," Article 25 of that Declaration says, "has the right to a standard of living adequate for the health and well-being of himself and his family, including food, clothing, housing and medical care."

Who wouldn't agree? Yet article 17 earlier qualifies, with two clauses: (1) "Everybody has the right to own property alone as well as in association with others"; and (2) "No one shall be arbitrarily deprived of his property." Articles 25 and 17 are both salient for any discussion of the right to the city. But aren't these two rights directly contradictory—contradictory in a bourgeois sense? The right to property deprives the poor of a place in the city, frequently a prominent place, perhaps even a center; yet nobody, apparently, can be deprived of their right to property, thus of their right to the city. Moreover, everybody has a right to adequate housing and well-being, but property owners have the private right to deny such a universal right, because no one can deprive them of their property. How to resolve this dilemma?

The dilemma is resolvable, or at least approachable, by going at it at once very specifically and very broadly, by homing in legally and opening out politically. By that I mean focusing on the specific grievance at hand, be it rent and lease hikes, be it problems of housing displacement, denial of public access to a particular urban space, police abuse, public "disorder" prosecutions, pre-emptive arrests of demonstrators, unlawful plainclothes infiltration of their groups, etc. There one might invoke "rights," such as human rights, constitutional rights or rights to the city, but what's needed is legal representation; one stands up for one's rights here in a legal sense, in a pragmatic sense, in an individual or collective sense. The other option, should this option fall on deaf ears, as invariably it does, is to open out the issue, mobilize politically, organize a campaign of Rebellion, en masse, a mass urban political movement, expressive of democratic yearnings.

These two routes aren't, of course, mutually exclusive. To be sure, they can go together, even go together concurrently. Meanwhile, if one wants to organize this two-pronged campaign under the general tagline RIGHT TO THE CITY, so be it: run with it, use that banner if it works tactically and practically. But can anyone really believe that in changing society or in understanding how society changes it helps one iota to discuss whether people exercise their rights or not? What matters most of all is surely whether people engage in *effective action*. And if actions are politically effective, we might want to pinpoint the conditions for their effectiveness. Not because those conditions are "rights," but because politically effective action is the crux of building any progressive movement. In my heart of hearts, movement building is what most concerns the chapters to follow, this book I put before you. In it, the new urban question signifies nothing less than the battle to invent another, upgraded notion of "collective consumption," a public prophylactic to the private parasites lurking in our midst.

Acknowledgements

My gratitude is extended to Anne Beech, David Harvey, Neil Brenner and Louis Moreno, without whom this book would not have been possible.

1

Whither Urban Studies?

In talking about urban studies, and about what's to follow in this book, I speak from and for the perspective I know best: the critical urban tradition that developed out of Marxism in the 1970s, as pioneered by the likes of Henri Lefebvre, David Harvey, and Manuel Castells. I tried to document and contribute toward this tradition in my book *Metromarxism*, where I claimed some of the best urban studies has been done by certain Marxists, and some of the best Marxism has been done by certain urban theorists.[1]

If we look back at the debates that raged in the 1970s, one of the biggest was about the nature of the urban. Just what is the urban anyway? What is a city? Why should it command such interest for critical scholars? The obvious rejoinder is that the city plays a special role under capitalism—indeed it was important in the birth of capitalism itself. The city assumes a twin role: an engine for capital accumulation, on the one hand, and a site for social/class struggle, on the other. It is crucial for the expansion of capitalism and for overthrowing capitalism. It is a theoretical object of curiosity because it is a political subject of necessity.

All of which bodes the question what is this "it"? In *The Urban Question*, Castells wondered what could we possibly mean by "city," and what is this concept "urban"? Why urban sociology and not simply sociology? Why urban geography and not simply geography? Castells, of course, was trying to figure out the specificity of the city, for both theory and politics, and it's a question we might still want to ponder. If anything, the question takes on renewed significance today because our world assumes a very different urban form than it did

1. Andy Merrifield, Metromarxism: *A Marxist Tale of the City*, Routledge, New York, 2002.

in the 1970s. Since 2006, the majority of the world's population is, we're told, urbanized, with some 3.3 billion dwellers living in urban agglomerations of some guise or another; and, if trends continue, this is set to increase exponentially. By 2030, 60 percent of planet earth will be urban; by 2050, 75 percent.

Yet beyond mere curiosity, what do these figures imply? Are they significant? Is urban studies a numbers game anyway? In 1938, the American sociologist Louis Wirth expressed a skepticism about "measuring" the degree to which the contemporary world is "urban" from the proportion of the total population living in cities. The influence cities exert upon social life, he said, is greater than any statistical population ratio might infer. The urban isn't a physical entity delimited in space but its very own *cosmos*, its very own "way of life."[2]

Never anyone terribly interested in numbers, Henri Lefebvre said a fuller understanding of our urban age could only be reached through conceptualization of the whole, through conceptualization of what he termed "planetary urbanization." In 1970, Lefebvre posited "the complete urbanization society."[3] In his day, he said, the complete urbanization of society was virtual, though one day might become real. Lefebvre is the last of a pretty extinct species: a philosopher of the city—or, better, "metaphilosopher" of the city.[4] This notion of "philosopher" harks back to the ancient Greeks; not somebody who is detached, solitary and contemplative, dealing with rarified abstractions, but somebody who's completely engaged in politics and big questions about democracy. Indeed, the very bedrock for ancient

2. Louis Wirth, "Urbanism as a Way of Life," *The American Journal of Sociology*, Volume 44, Number 1, July, 1938: 1–24.
3. Henri Lefebvre, *The Urban Revolution*, Minnesota University Press, Minneapolis, 2003.
4. Lefebvre was always rather slippery with his proclamations about metaphilosophy. He seems to suggest it is philosophizing beyond pure philosophy, a sort of free play with big concepts, with thoughts above and beyond philosophy, a philosophy without borders and limits, a holistic approach to social, existential, and political questions. His own brand of humanist Marxism is a metaphilosophy, a philosophy that realizes itself only through unified practice. Perhaps the greatest manifesto of metaphilosophy is Marx's eleven *Theses on Feuerbach*.

Greek philosophy was questions that linked the polis to democracy. The city, philosophy, and politics were synonymous. The philosopher Hippodamus, remember, was the first city planner, initially proposing a grid pattern and zoning scheme, as well as a central *agora* open square, that beloved place of gathering and assembly so precious to democracy; and we know how Plato, in *The Republic*, said much about how cities relate to democracy—or, as in Plato's case, to too much democracy.

The point here is that philosophy, the city, and political engagement all went together. Within the field of urban geography, particularly in U.K. urban geography, there are certain things that today militate against this noble philosophical tradition. One is the dominance of the positivist-empiricist tradition. The reason may be obvious in our age of "experts" and "technocrats," in this era some describe as "post-political": positivism has always hid behind the shield of quantification and "objectivity," always tried to rid itself of politics. In that sense, positivism/empiricism is a convenient methodology for technocrats trying to find consensus without conflict. Their opinions are neutral and expert, right? Their knowledge isn't value-laden. Yours, if it's critical and theoretically partisan, is warped, ideological.

The second reason for the prioritization of empirical data—which ties in neatly with the first reason—is that it can raise money for the corporate university, can more easily capture grant money, more easily produce a "knowledge commodity," a knowledge that may be calculated and evaluated in an institution's competitive yearnings and chart-topping desires. Very little money, if any, is doled out to work on theory, therefore theory/philosophy is unimportant because it is financially unimportant. To be sure, it is extremely difficult to evaluate and judge its "impact" on any spreadsheet.

You no longer think about a problem: you spend your time thinking about filling in a grant proposal about a problem. This creates a certain superficiality to the idea of doing "research": research constitutes amassing data; it rarely means thinking deeply about a problem, certainly not formulating concepts about this problem, and then engaging in a politics around that problem. This isn't helpful in the development of deeper, critical understandings of the urban problematic. Arguably, it creates a discipline that is at heart anti-intellectual. And anti-intellectualism doesn't "impact" well in the long run.

On the other flank, neither does sloppy theorizing, or theorizing divorced from political and social engagement. Consequently, there are dangers of "pure" theorizing, too, especially the sociologicalization of certain forms of continental philosophy, and here we might indict those who try to "adopt" or "instrumentalize" in some kind of disembodied way the usual suspects, thinkers like Badiou, Rancière, Žižek, Deleuze and Guattari, even Lefebvre. "Thoughts without content are empty," said Kant in *The Critique of Pure Reason*; although he also said "thoughts without concepts are blind." And so we hobble along, between analytical emptiness and conceptual blindness ...

* * *

Still, a reloaded urban studies doesn't mean middle-ground: it suggests a thorough reframing of the urban question, of dealing adequately with the *ontological* question, that of being in the world, of being in an urban world. Within this conceptualization we need to dispense with all the old chestnuts between global North and global South, between developed and underdeveloped worlds, between urban and rural, between urban and regional, between city and suburb, just as we need to dispense with old distinctions between public and private, state and economy, and politics and technocracy. From this standpoint, frontier lines don't pass between any North–South or urban–rural divide, but reside "within the phenomenon of the urban itself"—as Lefebvre says in *The Urban Revolution*. Hence the need to conceptualize and politicize how the globe is no longer demarcated through definitive splits between strict opposites: all demarcations and frontier lines are *immanent* within urban society, between dominated peripheries and dominating centers that exist all over the planet.

The notion of immanence is writ large in Marx's as well as Spinoza's thought, and is instructive for our own urban problematic. Immanence is everywhere in Marx's vocabulary. Marx said that *value* is immanent to capitalism, so is the *world market*, which is the very basis of capitalism, of what it is and what is emergent in its very Being; we could easily transpose "urban" for "world market" without losing any clarity of Marx's meaning. As for Spinoza, in *Ethics* he called the immanent force of nature and reality *substance*. Substance is the bedrock content to human reality, perceivable and conceivable only through its manifold *attributes*. Substance is, of course, Spinoza's pantheist theory of God, his notion that God is immanent in all reality, including ourselves; but maybe the form of this notion holds, too, for the immanent nature of the urban, for its complex ontological tissuing, for the fabric that now clothes our daily lives.

What is being affirmed here is the urban as a single substance whose attributes—the built environment, transport infrastructure, population densities, topographical features, social mixes, political governance—are all the formal *expressions* of what pervades it ontologically. We might even say that the "city" is an attribute of the urban. These attributes are how the urban looks and how it can be seen and known. The urban isn't out there, necessarily observable and measurable, but is immanent in our lives, an ontology *not an epistemology, not a transitive attribute of our society but the immanent substance of our society*.

Within this conceptualization, it's possible to conceive planetary urbanization not as simply bricks and mortar, as high-rise buildings and autoroutes, but as a process that produces skyscrapers as well as unpaved streets, highways as well as back roads, by-waters and marginal zones that feel the wrath of the world market—both its absence and its presence. This process involves dispossession of land, of sequestering the commons and eminent domain. The urban now signifies a new kind of "dependency," justifying cultural, technological and economic obsolescence in rural economies. In the 1970s, the peasant sociologist Andrew Pearse spoke of the expansion of an "Urban-Industrial-Complex" into the world's rural areas, which sanctioned agricultural production through an urban reward system. Today, we'd have to rename that complex an "Urban-Financial-Complex," with a reward system that penalizes and disciplines agricultural production, doing so planetarily, doing so from multiple centers of urban corporate power.[5]

---

5. Andrew Pearse, "Metropolis and Peasant: The Expansion of the Urban-Industrial-Complex and the Changing Rural Structure" in T. Shanin (ed.) *Peasants and Peasant Societies*, Penguin, Harmondsworth, 1971, p. 76.

* * *

We should stop using the term city, Lefebvre says, and adopt instead the terminology "urban society." Urban society, he was fond of saying, "is built upon the ruins of the city."[6] The city is a pseudo-concept, a historical concept, not an analytical reality. In pushing for the notion of urban society Lefebvre is asking us to open the floodgates, to quit bounding something, to give up on solidity and the security of an absolute and embrace something relative and open, something becoming. We should leave behind the form of the city and embrace the apparent formlessness of urban society.

I say "apparent" because we might remember there's nothing formless as such about Lefebvre's conception of space; he was keen to emphasize that space is global, fragmented and hierarchal in one fell swoop. It is a mosaic of stunning complexity, punctuated and textured by centers and peripheries, yet a mosaic in which the "commodity-form" gives this patterning its underlying definition. If we wanted to delve into the cell-like molecular structure of this urban substance, of this urban space, we could perhaps see it as an immense accumulation of commodities, bounded by the "commodity-form," even while its "value-form" is boundless. The "commodity-form" *vis-à-vis* the "value-form" is a key distinction Marx makes at the beginning of *Capital*. It was one way, after all, in which he could talk about how things have particularity and generality *at the same time*, have intrinsic form yet are also extrinsically formless. I'd like to see the urban pictured in the same analytical light, as something with structure and form, as something as functionally chaotic—Lefebvre's "rational delirium"—yet as fractally ordered as a series of subatomic particles.

We have to be imaginative about how we might conceive this reality. We could see it the way an atomic physicist might see it but really we are talking about something very vast—a terrestrial planetary universe. The commodity-form of space would represent the place-bound, fixed built-form, the built landscape that Sartre in *Critique of Dialectical Reason* called the "practico-inert." Meanwhile,

6. Henri Lefebvre, *Le droit à la ville*, Anthropos, Paris, 1968, p. 83.

the value-form would constitute a diffusive web of social
networked and stretched beyond place. If we wanted
further, the interaction between this value- and commodity-form is
a bit like the way Roquentin, the protagonist from Sartre's *Nausea*,
interacts with the world the inanimate objects, and the nausea that
that engenders for living, conscious beings: how this inanimate, fixed
world conditions and provides the passive frame for our active lives,
and how we must somehow render it dynamic. Now our nausea is
political and collective.

So within this conception, just *what* is the specificity of the urban, if indeed there is any specificity? There is and there isn't specificity, since it's a specificity of complementarity, an understanding that sees the urban as a complex circuit card, as a networked tissue, as clothing stitched together with pieces of delicate fabric. Outside of human woof and weft the urban creates nothing, is nothing. The urban serves no purpose and has no reality outside of human reality, outside of exchange and union, outside of human proximity and concentration, outside of human encounter and intensity. Nodes of intensity that resonate, that connect with other nodes of intensity, that fuse together and create energy and electricity, incandescent light.

"The signs of the urban," Lefebvre says in *The Urban Revolution*, "are signs of assembly: the things that promote assembly (streets, squares, spaces, surfaces, sidewalks, and buildings) and the requirements for assembly (seats, lights). The urban is most forcefully evoked by the constellation of lights at night, especially when flying over a city—the dazzling impression of brilliance, neon, street signs, streetlights, incitements of various kinds, the simultaneous accumulation of wealth and signs." The urban, Lefebvre says, is

> pure form: a place of encounter, assembly, simultaneity. This form has no specific content, but is a center of attraction and life. It is an abstraction, but unlike a metaphysical entity, the urban is a concrete abstraction, associated with practice. Living creatures, the products of industry, technology and wealth works of culture, ways of living ... Its contents (things, objects, people, situations) are mutually exclusive because they are diverse, but inclusive because they are brought together and imply their

> mutual presence. The urban is both form and receptacle, void and plenitude, super-object and non-object, supra-consciousness and the totality of consciousnesses.[7]

* * *

But why posit "urban society"? What's Lefebvre up to here, what's his point? Perhaps it isn't just an analytical trope he's deploying so much as a political strategy. Again, Spinoza can come to our aid. When he wrote *Ethics* and affirmed substance as the bedrock of life and nature, Spinoza coined three different kinds of knowledge. The first was the sort that occurred at the level of everyday life, with its chaos and disorder, a level totally legitimate and real for life yet an *inadequate* idea for fully understanding that life; the second kind of knowledge sees a bigger pattern of human *relationships* behind that chaos, understanding the interconnectivity of human life, the *common notions* that keep it together, intact, more or less. With a third kind of knowledge that understanding is pushed even further, to an intuitive reason of human experience, and here I am thinking that this might better describe urban life, our future becoming, the substance to our lives, the basis for improved and sustained common notions.

The major reason Spinoza developed this third kind of knowledge was because he saw something more fruitful at stake, something more open to human beings. He prioritized a reality that affirms its dependence and interdependence of all things, a tissue of collective belonging. Similarly, Henri Lefebvre thinks there's something more humanly fruitful and politically worthwhile in affirming his own third kind of knowledge: urban society. The capacity for extended and deepening common notions is thereby augmented, provided separations and segregations can be warded off, kept at bay. By reaching out to understand the common ingredients that bond us we can then reach inward to understand ourselves as both a people and individuals. Such is the promise of a "third kind" of urban knowledge. That seems to be Lefebvre's point; and even if it isn't, we should make this point for him.

---

7. Lefebvre, *The Urban Revolution*, pp. 118–9.

Lefebvre might have called this knowledge a "right to the city," but he also saw it as a new kind of citizenship, a revolutionary citizenship, based upon encounters between people, encounters that *reveal themselves though the negation of distance and though the reaching out to distance*. Citizenship is the point of convergence of both, a dialectic that is both a *perception* and a *horizon*, a structure of feeling as well as a new way of seeing ourselves and our planet. It is a citizenship conceived as something *urban*, as something territorial yet one in which territoriality is narrower and broader than both "city" and "nationality"; a citizen of the block, of the neighborhood, becomes a citizen of the world, a universal citizen rooted in place, encountering fellow citizens across the corridor and at the other end of the planet. Urbanization makes this sense of belonging possible, negating distance between everybody, piling people on top of one another, next to one another. Meanwhile, social media helps people reach out to distance, extend the distance of their lives, and the horizons of their ways of seeing, of seeing themselves and other people.

A new kind of citizenship might emerge out of this, an urban citizenship of workers without salaried work, of students without careers (the NINJA generation: "No Income, No Jobs and Assets"), of poor and middle-class people without homes, of retirees without pensions—a Here Comes Everybody (HCE) of people sharing a single planetary domain, one great big shit-pot together. In *La pensée marxiste et la ville*, Lefebvre expressed a simple formula: the more cities upsize and the more urban society emerges, the more steady salaried work will downsize.[8] Urban society will somehow be a "post-work" society in the sense that Marx hinted at in the *Grundrisse*, when we all eventually get "suspended" from the "immediate form of production," giving rise to a latent political constituency whose only real terrain left for struggle won't be the workplace but the urban itself.[9]

We're back again to the ancient Greeks—or maybe to the-not-so-ancient-Greeks—for whom politics was (is) always experienced

8. Lefebvre, *La pensée marxiste et la ville*, Casterman, Paris, 1972, especially Chapter II.
9. Cf. Marx, *Grundrisse*, Penguin, Harmondsworth, 1973, pp. 699–713.

and enacted in the urban *agora*; to that extent nothing much has changed under planetary urbanization, excepting that the *agora* has now gotten bigger and vaster—a virtual and physical world combined into one. Two and half thousand years ago the citizens of Athens didn't work; they were the aristocratic rulers who presided over the common folk—the slaves and strangers. Today, similarly, a new Greek citizenry emerges without work; not because they're aristocrats but because of economic crisis and eurozone austerity measures. Nowadays the *agora* is a new kind of "common field"—as Sartre might have said—in which the passivity of the world of corporate things, of the built financial landscape, of the spectacular "practico-inert," is rendered active and affective, doing so because it is filled with ordinary people who, united by common notions, create a function rather than respond to one (like a gaggle of shoppers).

Needless to say, there are people who fear this *agora*, who want to close it down physically, seal it off virtually, censor its cyberspace—the *agoraphobics*. But there are others who know that these days it isn't workers of the world who unite, who have a world to win, as Marx announced in the *Manifesto*; it's more that people have a whole world to occupy, to occupy as their own living space, their own sphere of reproduction. The agoraphobics constitute a ruling class in this planetary urbanization process, fractions of capital who are the "bearers" of the process of neo-Haussmannization; they're a global elite who put to shame the infamous Baron's spadework. Neo-Haussmannization now tears into the whole planetary urban fabric, and fronts the progressive production of core and periphery, of centers of power and wealth as well as spaces of dispossession and marginalization; and this everywhere, with little concern for either city or countryside.

Critical urban theory and philosophy must comprehend and create a new terrain for political interventions—for militant, revolutionary politics—in a process that is itself revolutionary. Indeed, "the urban" is revolutionary, Lefebvre says, and, as such, the revolution will be urban. That in a single line summarizes the gist of *The Urban Revolution*. It's a project that still lives on, in both directions. And a lot of conceptual and political steady work remains to be done in the right direction.

2

Old Urban Questions Revisited (and Reconstituted)

In 1972, when he first penned *La question urbaine* [*The Urban Question*], Manuel Castells was a spritely 28-year-old, a brilliant Spaniard in post-1968, revanchist Paris. That's pretty amazing stuff, this tender age, given the book's preeminence, given its enduring legacy as a "classic." The text was effectively Castells's doctoral dissertation done under the direction of Henri Lefebvre, on the one side, and sociologist Alain Touraine, on the other. We can put Lefebvre and Touraine on "either side" (and student Manuel in middle) because the two supervisors were themselves intellectual enemies. Touraine always thought Lefebvre overrated, too-loose a social scientific thinker; and Lefebvre never referenced Touraine's work anywhere. All of which stuck young Turk Castells between the rock and the hard place.

Touraine was a coiner of the notion of "post-industrial society," a gallic Daniel Bell; Lefebvre had, in turn, affirmed "the coming of urban society," which, if you read between the lines, was itself a sort of post-industrial thesis. Yet in order to put his own gloss on things, chart his own course between Scylla of Lefebvre and Charybdis of Touraine, where was young Manuel, a Marxist more empirical than Lefebvre and more theoretical than Touraine, to turn? How could he methodologically formalize his urban research while staying solidly Marxist? This was the early 1970s, and an obvious source for inspiration then was the dominant Marxist of the day, Louis Althusser.

Althusser was the master of brevity. What took Lefebvre whole books and more, Althusser laid down solid in 15 pages. Before long, Castells was mobilizing in original and idiosyncratic ways the twin pillars of Althusserian formalism: "Reproduction" and "Ideology." But, unlike Althusser himself, this was Althusserian formalism applied to the real world, to the conflictual urban condition of the 1970s, the fraught decade when capitalism was itself restructuring, attempting to shrug off the specter of post-war Fordist crisis and collapse. And although this urban system was declining, was in evident trouble, collapsing entirely it wasn't. Castells wanted to know why; and he wanted to illustrate that within the interstices of crisis came real possibilities for people, real possibilities to affirm themselves as urban citizens, as people who could actively shape their own urban destinies.

"Any child knows," Althusser says in one of his most brilliant essays "Ideology and Ideological State Apparatuses (Notes towards an Investigation)" (1969), "that a social formation which did not reproduce the conditions of production at the same time as it produced would not last a year."[1] The citation is a paraphrase of Marx, in a letter to Dr. Kugelmann (July 11, 1868), which summed up the whole point of Volume Two of *Capital*: without reproduction there could be no production; without the realization of surplus-value, no fresh surplus value could ever get produced; production is thus predicated on extended and expanded reproduction. Yet given the inevitable ruptures and disjunctures in the "normal" functioning of this capitalist process of production (outlined in Volume One of *Capital*), how was it that capitalism survived, still survives? How is it that the system is able to constantly reproduce itself?

Althusser suggests there are two key aspects of this reproduction process for Marx: (1) Reproduction of the means of production (Marx's Departments I from Volume Two of *Capital*); and (2) Reproduction of labor-power (Marx's Department II from Volume Two of *Capital*), of which there's a three-pronged sub-category (a) wages; (b) unproductive consumption, like housing, schooling, hospitals, etc.; and (c) ideology: compliance to the dominant order, accepting all this as "normal" and somehow "natural," that is it like this and only like this.

It's curious that Althusser passes over stuff about the reproduction of capitalist relations of production from Volume Two of *Capital*,

1. Louis Althusser, *Lenin and Philosophy and Other Essays*, New Left Books, London, 1971.

passes over those political-economic "reproduction schemas" that Marx conceptualizes (Departments I as well as II). Instead, he beds his vision down in the *ideological* reproduction of labor-power, a theme Marx doesn't tackle head on. "We shall not go into the [political-economic] analysis of this question," Althusser says of Volume Two of *Capital*. "It is enough to have mentioned the existence of the necessity of the reproduction of the material conditions of production." And so Althusser bases everything on his particular notion of ideology, on "the imaginary representation of an individual's real conditions of existence."

Ideology, for Althusser, just like the unconscious for Freud, has no history. Yet it does have material existence: it *really* is embodied in both the "Ideological State Apparatuses" (ISAs) and "Repressive State Apparatuses" (RSAs). ISAs, for instance, are educational institutions, the family, mass media, the church and religious associations, political parties, and trade unions. These are all institutions that function through ideology, that somehow perpetuate ideology. They "hail" (*interpellate*) individuals as distinctive *subjects*, recruit us as compliant members of capitalist society; that's one way in which "the system" reproduces its legitimacy and order. "Hey you, there!" says Althusser, as somebody yells from across the street, somebody we instinctively know is shouting us, hailing us. We know it's us they mean; we cannot choose but hear and look. Ideology, says Althusser, works in much the same vein. And if we choose not to look, not to hear, to free ourselves from this ideological hailing, then the RSAs (with its police, military, and law courts) step in to force us to look and listen, compelling us to be obedient stiffs in this capitalistic melodrama.

Castells makes use of these twin themes of reproduction and ideology in his urban research in vital ways, in original ways. Indeed, for him there's something similar going on in the urban realm. For a start, the urban system—or "urban structure," as Castells calls it—reproduces itself despite crisis; it did back then and still does it now. How so? Well, says Castells, because of ideology, because of how ideology operates insidiously within this system, and operates in detrimental ways within the scholarly field of urban studies, too. In each instance it hails us as compliant objects not as active role-playing subjects who script the performance. Castells attacks urban studies and urban sociology precisely for its ideological content. Erstwhile research on "the city" has formulated "imaginary representations," he says, framing the city in terms of "urban culture," in narrow sociological and anthropological terms. Such approaches focus on "dimensions of the city," on "densities," "size," on the idea that the city exhibits a particular specificity, its own of organization and transformation; a logic which, says Castells, pays scant attention to broader dynamics of capitalist political-economic and social relations. As Castells argues, "the laws of articulation and transformation" of the urban system are discovered in the spatial forms of capitalist social structure as a whole. To deny this is to create an ideological representation of the urban question, an imaginary representation.

Thus arose one of the chief problematics in *The Urban Question*: given we need to define a non-ideological understanding of urbanism, what, then, might constitute this reality we call "the urban"? And what, from a Marxist standpoint, is "urban politics"? How is the urban a distinctive "object" of analysis as well as a special arena of political struggle? How, in other words, can you define the urban as a specific theoretical and political question? *Voilà la question urbaine ...*

Castells's response was both brilliant and flawed, brilliant in how he utilized Althusser, flawed in how the thesis had a hard time reproducing itself beyond the 1980s. For in *The Urban Question* Castells says the urban isn't a unit of production; production operates at a bigger scale, at a regional and international scale. Thus production isn't the right analytical entry point into the urban question. Rather, it is, à la Althusser, *reproduction* that counts most, the reproduction of the urban system and its links to the overall survival of capitalism. The urban, to adopt Castells's own intricate definition, is "a specific articulation of the instances of the social structure within a spatial unit of the reproduction of labor-power."[2] The urban, in short—if it's ever possible to put it "in short" with Castells—is crucial in production and expanded reproduction of the mode of production. But, in doing so, it opens up a whole new and more expansive domain of crisis and contradiction, and of political engagement.

2. Castells, *The Urban Question*, p. 237.

From the mid-1970s onwards, Castells began to define and refine his notion of the urban as the spatial unit of what he'd call "collective consumption." Collective consumption is implicit in the reproduction of "unproductive" collective goods and services outside of the wage-relation, outside of variable capital, namely public housing, public infrastructure, transport infrastructure, schools, and hospitals, and collectively-consumed services. "It is in this sense," Castells says,

> that the essential problems regarded as urban are in fact bound up with the processes of "collective consumption," or what Marxists call the organization of the collective means of reproduction of labor-power. That is to say, means of consumption objectively socialized, which, for specific historical reasons, are essentially dependent for their production, distribution and administration on the intervention of the state. This is no arbitrary definition. It is a working hypothesis that may be verified by the concrete analysis of advanced capitalist societies—and this is what I have set out to do.[3]

* * *

So, here, we arrive at Castells's understanding of urban politics: an intervention in this reproductive process, an intervention made by the state, on the one hand, funding these public goods, orchestrating urban planning and policy, figuring out the whole ideological and material organization of space and social conditions of the reproduction of labor-power; and, on the other hand, inventions made by ordinary people, who collectively contest state intervention, who engage politically with the state in its organization, in its management and mismanagement of collective consumption. Enter *urban social movements*, citizen alliances and grassroots groups who're relative autonomous from ideological party politics. Activism henceforth cuts across class lines and unfolds not at workplace but in the living space, in the neighborhood, in the realm of reproduction—

3. Castells, *The Urban Question*, p. 440.

or, better, in the realm where reproduction meets production, that vast and intimate arena Lefebvre termed "everyday life."

Throughout the 1970s such an understanding became a working hypothesis of *The Urban Question*, tried, tested, and refined against a backdrop of crisis-ridden reality: financial crisis (breakdown of the Bretton Woods agreement, 1971), oil crisis (1973), fiscal crises of the state (circa 1975), the "Winter of Discontent" (Britain, circa 1978). At every level of jurisdiction, and almost everywhere, the state began divesting from collective consumption budgets, and, in response, urban social movements began sprouting up almost everywhere, demanding sustainable affordable housing, functioning mass transit, decent schools, reliable public services. What arose over that decade—"the repugnant 1970s," Guy Debord once branded it—was a strange and conflictual predicament for progressive people: items of collective consumption so vital for reproduction of the relations of production, so vital for freeing up "bottlenecks" in the system, so vital for providing necessary (yet unprofitable) goods and services, so indispensable for propping up demand in the economy—were now being cast aside. How could this be? What once appeared essential ingredients for capitalism's continued reproduction—for its long-term survival—turned out to be only contingent after all; the state began desisting from coughing up money for them; and soon, as the 1980s kicked in, would actively and ideologically wage war against them.

Of course, items of collective consumption were always ideologically loaded anyway: they maintained the status quo, were a sop, a special form of social pacification, keeping dominant social relations in place; they were a crippling and stifling form of dependency that crushed peoples' activity and entrepreneurship in civil society. And yet, more disturbingly, what to do when they're being taken away? Source of problem or harbinger of possibility? Likely both for the dialectician.

The left has never come to terms with the shock waves this earthquake engendered; the seismic tremor that registered big digits on the neoliberal Richter Scale. One immediate response back then was "Eurocommunism," the "democratic road to socialism," which became *de rigueur* during the 1970s in continental European left camps, and, a bit later, during the 1980s, in Britain (e.g. municipal socialism in London, Sheffield, and Liverpool). This was also the moment when Castells seemed to change his political heart and analytical tack: from the "hyper-formalism" of Althusserian Marxism, to an embracing of Nicos Poulantzas's concept of the state as the "condensation" of class forces; a reality where the state isn't divorced from real people, a higher power beyond real people, nor a simple instrument of capital. Rather, the Poulantzian state is precisely comprised of ordinary people, people of differing political persuasions and loyalties, and not all of them tied to reproducing the bureaucratic status quo. The state's corridors and agencies are themselves sites of social and class struggle. The state is a complex, messy, "relatively-autonomous" institution that can be infiltrated from without and usurped from within—all for the common good. Or so it was thought.[4]

The promise of Eurocommunism was that it might prop up what David Harvey has recently called "the rebel city." Yet the reality of the movement was something different again: during the 1980s protagonists frequently collapsed and capitulated in face of rabid free-marketeers, or else became rabid free-marketeers themselves. Zealot Eurocommunists and compadre social democratic state bureaucrats (including not a few '68ers) suddenly began morphing into a new hybrid breed: neoliberal entrepreneurial managers (Mitterrand's reign was full of them; his French presidency became paradigmatic in this peculiar shift). Entrepreneurial managers and managerial entrepreneurs turned into a new species of ardent proponents of what Castells himself would label "the wild city," pushing through more subtle transformations that occurred within neoliberalism's birth-pangs—alongside Thatcher's and Reagan's Caesarean slashes.

The wild city meant the deregulated city, the downsized city, downsized in the sense that capitalist production downsizes, trimming and sometimes slashing its budgets and workforce; only here it was whole municipalities laying off workers and cutting

---

4. The best example of Castells's Eurocommunist moment was his book *City, Class and Power* (Macmillan, London, 1978).

back public services. All of which dramatized a city whose identity assumes the status of a "lean" corporate enterprise, forever eyeing the bottom-line, measuring itself typically by its ability to balance its books, to operate efficiently, to maximize its service provision at minimum cost. The threshold, of course, was simply what city governments could get away with, get away with while still remaining in office, still maintaining legitimacy with their electorate. In the wild city—with its dynamic of "lean urbanization" (as I called it in my book *Dialectical Urbanism*[5])—municipal councils mimic corporate boardrooms; city and national governments outsource themselves, launch competitive bidding for public service contracts—with the cheapest bid usually winning; more attention is always paid to Moody's and other Wall Street investment rating agencies than to real peoples' needs.

What we didn't realize back then, yet know now, is that the wild city is really what Henri Lefebvre was all along calling "urban society"; in fact, the wild city resembles a microcosmic instant of what Lefebvre saw as "planetary urbanization," a process whereby metropolitan expansion becomes hyper-exploitative and hyper-expansive; not least because cities burst out of their shells, have their regulatory fetters removed and float themselves on the world free-market for urbanization. Soon not only would ruling elites pioneering this process divest from collective consumption budgets; they'd actively dispossess former items of collective consumption as well, like public utilities and public infrastructure. When he wrote *The Urban Question* Castells could never have imagined this state of affairs, an affair of the state desisting from its responsibilities *vis-à-vis* social reproduction. Yet the state did turn its back on the subsidization of people in favor of the subsidization of capital, concentrating on the reproduction of "productive" consumption, even if "productive" here in no way implies actual production. As it unfolded in the 1980s and 1990s, and as it stands today, extended reproduction of capital is achieved through financialization and dispossession, through dispossession and reconfiguration of urban space.

5. Andy Merrifield, *Dialectical Urbanism: Social Struggles in the Capitalist City*, Monthly Review Press, New York, 2002.

* * *

Where, then, does that leave us? The urban question of Castells, we might say, is, in response, now the *old* urban question. Defining the urban as a spatial unity of collective consumption no longer holds. It may be brutal to admit, but *The Urban Question* is a dated book, at least in its content, even if its form continues to pose pertinent questions about the urban question, about what urban politics can and ought to be, about how it relates to scuppering capitalist reproduction. Rereading Althusser's ISA essay, it's noteworthy how Althusser, like Castells, made short shrift of the "reproduction of relations of production" that Marx sketched out in Volume Two of *Capital*. Yet maybe it's here, in this process of reproduction of capital, on a planetary scale, where progressive political interventions must take place? How to affirm *democracy*, how to intervene in the reproduction of relations of productive consumption, infiltrate capitalism's capillaries and arteries of financial power and neo-Haussmannite administration? How to do that rather than make defensive demands for public resources long since privatized?

The latter is now a *fait accompli*. There's no going backward to good old days of the public sector, to the old paternal state, to the providential state that seemed to care about people. This shock of recognition, painful as it is, closely follows the Marxism of *The Communist Manifesto*, a Marxism that moves with capitalism's melting vision, that gets inside this vision and actuality, that goes forward though this vision. It doesn't live in denial of this state of affairs: it is a Marxism that revolutionizes itself by revolutionizing the urban. As Harvey himself said in the closing lines of *Social Justice and the City*, a book now over 40 years young: "It remains for revolutionary theory to chart the path from an urbanism based in exploitation to an urbanism appropriate for the human species. And it remains for revolutionary practice to accomplish such a transformation."[6]

One of the major points of divergence between Castells's *The Urban Question* and Harvey's *Social Justice and the City*, and why

6. David Harvey, *Social Justice and the City*, University of Georgia Press, Athens, GA, [1973] revised edition 2009, p. 314.

the latter book has had a longer radical shelf life, is that the city in Harvey's analysis assumes a much more dynamic significance. It is a *productive* rather than reproductive instrument within capitalism, an active staging rather than reactive scenery. When Castells speaks of reproduction of labor-power and of affordable housing and neighborhood public services within the basic dynamics of social reproduction, Harvey is keen to emphasize urban land as a commodity, as a site for the appropriation of class-monopoly rents; the city, from this standpoint, is itself exchange value, ripe for stock market valorization and investment portfolio exploitation.

Some of the most provocative parts of *Social Justice and the City* are where Harvey (in 1973) takes on neoclassical theories of urban land use, bringing Marx and class relations to bear on aspects that had hitherto been seen as mere "factors of production." From this standpoint, *land*, *labor*, and *capital* aren't conceived as mere things, but are, respectively, *landlords*, *workers*, and *capitalists*, actual living bearers of processes, whose roles are conflictual and frequently conflated within urban political-economy. The shift in terminology to class relations and social conflict was more politically profounder then than it might sound now. For Harvey had ushered in a harder-edged "revolutionary" theory, denouncing old urban theories as at best "liberal," at worst "counter-revolutionary," as actively obfuscating and intentionally ideological (though never admitting it); and this because of their pretensions to science and "objectivity." Harvey's inspiration was—still is—classical Marxism, a more thematic than symptomatic reading of Marxism, more grounded than formalistic, more *Capital* (three volumes) than *Reading Capital* (one volume).

"In capitalist economies," says Harvey, "rent arises in monopoly, differential and absolute forms. Once it has arisen, rent serves to allocate land to uses ... But when value determines use, the allocation takes place under the auspices of rampant speculation, artificially induced scarcities, and it loses any pretense of having anything at all to do with the efficient organization of production and distribution." "Unfortunately," Harvey continues, typically contentiously,

> the monopolistic power of private property can be realized in its economic form by innumerable stratagems. If rent cannot

> be extracted by one means then it will by another. Social policy, no matter how well-intentioned, is helpless in the face of these innumerable stratagems—the rentier will get that pound of flesh no matter what. It is this fact, however, that lends a certain homogeneity to capitalist city forms in spite of quite marked differences from country to country (and even from city to city) in political, legal and administrative institutions, as well as in production, distribution and the social matrix in the community.[7]

This understanding posed—goes on posing—tough questions for theory as well as for politics, especially for politics, for politics struggling for a socially just urbanism. Urban theory has to deal with "things" in the urban neighborhood, with the concrete urban "use" values that Castells identified, stuff that really does concern social reproduction and grounded activism; yet politics must do so while fending off, and attacking, the dynamics of capital circulating into specific built urban environments, how it flows as "the secondary circuit of capital" chasing class-monopoly ground rents across the globe. Theory and politics, in other words, must deal with the reality of what Harvey in *The Limits to Capital* (1982) would, after the Marx of Volume Three of *Capital*, call "fictitious capital."

Fictitious capital is the motive force of the secondary circuit of capital. Fictitious capital is quite literally this circulatory process in its most fluid state of becoming. Becoming what? Becoming the realized form of surplus value, the realization of real rental income. A "title to land," says Harvey, "becomes a form of fictitious capital"; money capital doled out is equivalent to an interest-bearing investment, a claim upon anticipated future revenues, a future gain. Fictitious capital, though, implies nothing unreal because it has a deep materiality, a very real existence. "Ground-rent," Harvey says, "when capitalized as the interest on some imaginary capital, constitutes the real 'value' of the land."[8] Commenting on *Limits*—a "magisterial review and re-theorization of Marx"—Fredric Jameson says

---

7. Harvey, *Social Justice and the City*, pp. 190–1.
8. David Harvey, *The Limits to Capital*, Verso, London, 1999, p. 367.

> Harvey suggests that for Marx the value of land is something like a structurally necessary fiction ... This is possible only because fictitious capital is oriented towards the expectation of future value: and thus with one stroke the value of land is revealed to be intimately related to the credit system, the stock market and finance capital generally.[9]

Real estate functions as a "second circuit of capital," as a circuit that runs parallel to that of industrial production, to the primary circuit of capital, one serving as a buffer, as a site where capital flows in the event of a depression. Yet as the primary circuit begins to slow down, as it begins to downsize, as it *has* slowed down, capital increasingly shifts to the secondary circuit. Soon it supplants the primary circuit in relative importance within the overall money-making economy—though with destabilizing implications. Here Harvey treads a lot further with the Lefebvrian hypothesis from *The Urban Revolution*. He tests it out, unpacks it, deepens it. If we were to unpack the process, unpack it as Harvey unpacks it in *Limits*, fictitious capital flows in the secondary circuit with three distinctive metamorphoses, transformative states that follow the three states of circulating capital emphasized in Volume Two of *Capital*: namely, *money* capital, *productive* capital and *commodity* capital. Money is lent by a financier as interest-bearing capital to a property developer and/or real estate company, who act as the bearer of "productive capital," as capital creating a physical form somewhere, as a merchant capitalist who will sell the finished spatial commodity (a building, for example) for a price higher than it cost to produce it; or else they might—as rentier capitalists—hold on to the asset to generate incremental rents, whilst servicing their debt with a lender. Though, invariably, lenders and rentiers are one and the same person, one and the same organization or institution—again showing how rental markets and stock markets are intimately related, far too related for their own good. That said, the point at which fictitious capital accumulates rental income is the point at which fictitious capital is no longer fictitious: it is there

9. Fredric Jameson, "The Brick and the Balloon: Architecture, Idealism and Land Speculation," *New Left Review*, No. 228, March–April 1998, pp. 42–3.

and then *commodity* capital, there and then fixed capital, a cold and tangible practico-inert.

The Limits to Capital advanced with greater theoretical sophistication the bold "Conclusions and Reflections" that closed *Social Justice and the City*. It was almost a decade in the coming, propelling urban theory into the 1980s, into a new regime of urban governance, one *Limits* largely prefigured. Once, in the 1960s and 1970s, "managerialism" prevailed, functioned through demand-side collective consumption; from the 1980s onwards, "entrepreneurialism" and supply-side subsidization became the new tagline. Life had caught up: Harvey's theory of land as a pure financial asset quickly came into its own explanatory glory, comprehending what is today real empirical reality, a real bourgeois-driven tragedy; a tragedy I've been calling *neo-Haussmannization*.

Neo-Haussmannization would be impossible to imagine if land hadn't taken on the pure character of fictitious capital, had it not assumed the status of interest-bearing capital, circulating through the property market, enhancing the value of land, redeveloping and upscaling that land for "higher" and "better" capitalistic uses—for higher exchange values, gleaned as class-monopoly rent. Harvey puts it succinctly in *The Limits to Capital*:

> the circulation of interest-bearing capital promotes activities on the land that conform to the highest and best uses, not simply in the present, but also in anticipation of future surplus value production. The landowners who treat the land as a pure financial asset perform exactly such a task ... By looking to the future, they inject a fluidity and dynamism into the use of land that would otherwise be hard to generate.

And yet, "the freer interest-bearing capital is to roam the land looking for future ground-rents to appropriate...and the more open the land market is, the more recklessly can surplus money capital build pyramids of debt claims and seek to realize its excessive hopes through the pillaging and destruction of production on the land itself."[10]

10. Harvey, *The Limits to Capital*, pp. 368–9.

* * *

Where Manual Castells and David Harvey do actually converge is around the notion of reproduction. Where this convergence diverges is in the *nature* of such reproduction. For Castells, reproduction is, above all else, social reproduction, reproduction of labor-power, reproduction in the sense that Althusser outlines it. The urban, we've heard, is for Castells a spatial unit of collective reproduction of labor-power; urban politics is the collective political intervention in this reproductory process, an engagement wherein urban social movements battle over retaining collective consumption, even try to self-manage collective consumption. For Harvey, reproduction means *reproduction of capital*, reproduction in the sense that Marx outlined it in Volume Two of *Capital*. The urban, for Harvey, gets defined by how capital circulates into land markets and how it produces (and gets imprisoned by) an agglomeration of fixed assets. Urban politics unfolds as a collective intervention in this reproductory process, a process marked by discontinuity and disruption, by crisis and social conflict; the enigma of capital—and the enigma *for* capital—is how these glitches and breakdowns can be resolved, sorted out, managed.[11]

In *The Limits to Capital* (p.371), Harvey says the state "is the final line of defense." The state, he says, is equipped with all sorts of power to regulate land use; to expropriate land; to plan land use; to invest in land use; to subsidize capital and safety-net capital over land use. Over 30 years on, one might wonder if this notion of "defense"

---

11. Harvey has recently penned his *Companion to Marx's Capital Volume Two* (Verso, London, 2013) to emphasize how the essence of capital is indeed fraught with glitches and disjunctures. *Capital Volume One*, Harvey says, concerns itself with the production of surplus-value, whereas *Capital Volume Two* focuses on the realization of this surplus-value. Marx's major message, of course, is the inextricable unity of the production and realization of surplus-value, which marks the total reproductory process. It's a passionate lovers' embrace, however, whose "true course," Marx knows, "never runs smooth." The inevitable friction, Harvey thinks, provides a moment of great threat and trauma, as well as immanent political possibility. Where Harvey's contribution is so brilliant, is in countering Engels' claim that *Capital Volume Two* hasn't got much grist for "political agitation."

warrants an upgrade? Indeed, these days, insofar as the business of capital management goes, insofar as the business of addressing glitches within the overall reproduction of capital in the economy goes, the state is more a *first* line of defense, a veritable executive committee for managing the common affairs of a bourgeoisie and aristocratic super-elite, stepping in at the *first* signs of crisis, baling out the bankrupted corporations, the debt-ridden financial institutions, dishing out corporate welfare to multinationals, turning a blind-eye to tax avoidance and sleazy accountancy. One way in which the state has gotten away with it in contemporary climes is through "austerity governance," through "rule by accountancy": to balance municipal and federal books, family treasures have been sold off, public sector assets privatized, service management contracted-out; and land has generally been given away or sold at lowly fire-sale prices. As such, and as Jamie Peck recently put it, "the systematic dumping of risks, responsibility, debts and deficits" removes the onus from the corporate and financial sector, off-loading this onus onto local states and local ordinary taxpaying people. This is partly how the "enigma" of capital reproduction hasn't so much been resolved as displaced, temporarily diffused. And here, as Peck again says, "austerity has become a strategic space for the contradictory reproduction of market rule."[12]

Still, there's another flank here, the flank that interests Harvey and the flank that interests me most of all in this book: the *enigma of revolt*, the possibilities for people collectively to intervene in this process, a process that isn't necessarily about creating an urban social movement as kick-starting a political movement that's urban-based, that somehow grounds itself in the urban—urban in its broadest and deepest sense. To a large degree, the urban politics of Manuel Castells are a lot more straightforward than those of David Harvey. The former sees politics as engaging with the state as much as with capital, as subverting and re-appropriating state power, as demanding collective public goods, as rallying for relatively autonomous self-management of these public goods. For Harvey, the urban takes on a much broader

12. Jamie Peck, "Austerity Urbanism," *City: Analysis of Urban Trends, Culture, Theory, Policy, Action*, Vol. 16, No. 6, 2012, pp. 626–55.

reach and more ambitious remit: it is an arena for larger intervention, an arena whereby the whole domain of the extended reproduction of capital needs to be contested. Those flows of interest-bearing capital prop up the secondary circuit; they go frantically chasing rents in a global urbanization boom, in the global neo-Haussmannization that currently underwrites this urbanization boom. Interest-bearing capital helps create the fixed assets and the built environment that forms the physical manifestation of the city, the Spinozian *attributes* of the city. But the realm of politics needs to deal with the *substance* of these attributes, the way in which they enter daily life, how they materialize and undermine that daily life. And, as we'll see in the chapters to come, this political space is nothing other than the urban itself, the real and normative battleground in which a new urban question continues to impose itself in evermore rapacious guises and disguises.

3

Cities Under Tension

> The form of a city changes quicker, alas, than the human heart.
>
> —Baudelaire

> I am tempted to the belief that what are called necessary institutions are only institutions to which one is accustomed, and that in matters of social constitution the field of possibilities is much wider than people living within each society imagine.
>
> —Alexis de Tocqueville

In a remarkable series of essays, bundled together under the rubric *Paris sous tension*, popular historian and organic intellectual Eric Hazan sings a paean for his hometown under fire, his *Paris under tension*; the pressure gauge is edging toward danger level and seems about to blow anytime.[1] Hazan, who trained as a cardiologist and in the 1970s worked as a surgeon in poor Palestinian refugee camps in the Lebanon, now fronts the left publishing house he founded in 1998, La fabrique. He takes leave from one of Balzac's remarks: "old Paris is disappearing with a frightening rapidity." Yet while Hazan's pages are full of a long lineage of Parisians who, like Balzac, lamented this disappearance—Hugo, Chateaubriand, Baudelaire, Chevalier, Debord—he's over his grief for a lost loved one; he's sobered up, detests nostalgia, and embraces a future that looks a lot different from a once glorious past.

In this sequel to *L'invention de Paris* (2002) [*The Invention of Paris*],[2] Hazan evokes another Paris, a popular Paris; his dandies and *flâneurs*

---

1. Eric Hazan, *Paris sous tension*, Éditions la fabrique, Paris, 2011.
2. Eric Hazan, *L'invention de Paris: Il n'y a pas de pas perdus*, Éditions du Seuil, Paris, 2002; also *The Invention of Paris: A History in Footsteps*, Verso, London, 2010. The English version transforms Hazan's original subtitle, which plays

have darker skins and many don't speak native French; his Paris lies beyond the center, is even a Paris without a center, one he invents in his head and out on the streets. (Is there any living urbanist who knows their city so intimately? Hazan seems to know all the names on doorbells, let alone buildings and inner courtyards.) Hazan bids adieu to the dead Paris *inside* the *boulevard périphérique*, regretting nothing and seemingly fearing nothing. His Paris isn't the two million denizens of the predominantly white, bourgeois core, dancing to the tune of greedy real estate interests on the one side, and a spectacular tourist market—a Disneyland for the cultivated—on the other, each consciously and unconsciously conspiring to rid the grand capital of the poor.

It's assorted *banlieues* that hold the collective key, the outer "red belts" of eight million predominantly black and Arab peoples, throbbing with sometimes scary and impoverished life yet always hustling on the edge. Forever the optimist, Hazan sees all this as the source of great energy and potential for renewed urban vitality; this is where a new radiant Paris will re-emerge, if it ever re-emerges. Forget about the center. Parisian ruling classes have banished so many people to the outside that now the periphery is somehow central to the city's urban future, to an urban form beyond the traditional city norm. Tourists come to gape at Paris's lovely museums, at the museumified *quartiers*, at the beautiful buildings and monuments, at an entombed, cold history; but the real living history, the real Paris as a living organism, breathing and palpitating, ain't so regal, and lies beyond the breach, beyond Pompidou's peripheral barrier. Even so, amid these changes some things don't change: "my conviction," says Hazan, "is that Paris still is what it has been for two-centuries: a great battleground of a civil war between aristocrats and *sans-culottes*."[3]

* * *

on André Breton's *Nadja* [1928]. "Lost Steps?" wonders Nadja, after Breton gives her his book *Les pas perdus* [Lost Steps]. "Mais il n'y en a pas" ["But there aren't any"], she declares. There is no such thing as lost steps in Paris ... .

3. Hazan, *Paris sous tension*, p. 10.

Hazan mightn't know it—though I suspect he does—but what he's sketching out here is a new urban question. It's new—or relatively new—for two reasons. The first is how Paris, we know, gave us that prototypical urban practice in the 1850s—Haussmannization—an infamous process of divide and rule, of class expulsion through spatial transformation, of social polarization through economic and political gerrymandering. It was a ruthless counter-revolution that tore into medieval Paris and old working-class neighborhoods, mobilizing public monies to prime the private real estate pump, enabling investors to find new speculative outlets in the built landscape of the city. The sense of loss, the sense of dispossession, was apparent for many poor Parisians and is still felt by their counterparts 150 years down the line. Though today Paris is no longer paradigmatic but microcosmic of a new process of divide and rule, a new global process: neo-Haussmannization.

Haussmannization and neo-Haussmannization share a historical and geographical lineage. But the primal scene of its progeny needs updating and upgrading. Those grand boulevards still flow with people and traffic, even if the boulevard is now reincarnated in the highway, and that highway is more often at a standstill, log-jammed at every hour. Twenty-first-century grand boulevards now flow with energy and finance, with information and communication, and they're frequently fiber-optic and digitalized, ripping through cyberspace as well as physical space. Neo-Haussmannization is a global-urban strategy that has peripheralized millions of people everywhere to the extent that it makes no sense anymore to talk about these peoples being peripheral. As cities have exploded into mega-cities, and as urban centers—even in the poorest countries—have gotten de-centered, glitzy and internationalized, "Bonapartism" projects its urban tradition onto planetary space.

What's happening in Paris, then, is a revealing microcosm of a larger macrocosm. Paris is a cell-form of a bigger urban tissuing that's constituted by a mosaic of centers and peripheries scattered all over the globe, a patchwork quilt of socio-spatial and racial apartheid that goes for Paris as for Palestine, for London as for Rio, for Johannesburg as for New York. Differences are differences of degree not substance, not in the essential unity of process, engineered as it is by a global ruling class intent on business. Nowadays, the poor global South exists in northeast Paris, or in Queens and Tower Hamlets. And the rich global North lives high above the streets of Mumbai, and flies home in helicopters to its penthouses in Jardins and Morumbi, São Paulo.

This spatial apartheid has now begotten a new paradox in which centers and peripheries oppose one another; the fault lines and frontiers between the two worlds aren't some straightforward urban–suburban divide, nor necessarily anything North–South. Rather, centers and peripheries are *immanent* within global accumulation of capital, *immanent* within the "secondary circuit of capital." Profitable locations get pillaged as secondary circuit flows become torrential, just as other sectors and places are asphyxiated through disinvestment. Therein centrality creates its own periphery, crisis-ridden on both flanks. The two worlds—center and periphery—exist side-by-side, everywhere, cordoned off from one another, everywhere.

The second theme that Hazan mischievously pinpoints, following just as immanently from the first, is *insurrection*, one of his favorite words. Little surprise that La fabrique first made public that most incendiary of insurrectional tracts, *L'insurrection qui vient* [*The Coming Insurrection*].[4] (After its publication in 2007 and the subsequent arrest of the "Tarnac Nine," anti-terrorist police called Hazan in for questioning at *Le quai des orfèvres*, subjecting him to four hours of abusive interrogation about the author's identity. He remained tight-lipped throughout.) Hazan's idea about insurrection is twin-pronged (even if he never says so explicitly), dramatized by both an *inner* energy and an *outer* compulsion—or, rather, an outer propulsion.

The inner energy is a burning desire to live on the margins, to rebuild the margins, to make one's neighborhood a livable neighborhood—the center of one's life. It's a familiar immigrants tale, even if these immigrants are sometimes born in this foreign land and carry its passport. In certain peripheral Parisian spaces, Hazan

4. *Comité invisible*, *L'insurrection qui vient*, Éditions la fabrique, Paris, 2007; also The Invisible Committee, *The Coming Insurrection*, Semiotext(e), Los Angeles, CA, 2009.

spots the germ of an artisanal, spontaneous and collective rebuilding program in action, reminiscent of what's going on in Ramallah. There's even something inventive happening in the core, too, at the corner of rue Morand and rue de l'Orillon in the XIe arrondissement, he says, involving Arab and Malian masons and carpenters who scavenge breeze-block and wood and bricks from God knows where to quasi-legally rehab an entire building. Atypical for Paris, the architecture is vernacular rather than spectacular, serving local needs and nobly integrating itself within a "healthy" urban tissuing. (An ex-surgeon, Hazan knows all about dead and live tissue.)

Here we have the urban as use-value not exchange-value, as a lived not ripped off realm, with integrative not speculative housing; it's a project, too, that has plenty of scope for scaling up after the insurrection, after an inner energy to rebuild erupts into an expansive and propulsive momentum to democratize. In that sense it's very likely, Hazan thinks, that *l'insurrection qui vient* won't erupt in central Paris: The coming insurrection will erupt on the periphery, out on the global periphery, where dispossessed and marginalized denizens—"the dangerous classes"—will organize and mobilize themselves to create a truly "popular" urbanism, generating at the same time tensions at the centers they surround; and maybe, just maybe, one day actually "recuperating" that center. Hazan doesn't speak of a "right to the city" as his organizing banner. For him, it's the *political* insurrection that finds its expression in any outer propulsion; not a desire to change the government or the municipality, but to change the existing nature of society—"to change life," as Lefebvre might have said.

* * *

Nowhere in *Paris sous tension* does Hazan adopt the vocabulary of "Occupy," either; but it's not too hard to nudge him along in that direction. Like Occupy, Hazan's notion of insurrection represents a *hypothesis*, a daring hunch that, for people who care about democracy, for people who know our economic and political system is kaput, change is likely to come from within, from within excluded and impoverished communities, through collective experimentation and struggle, through action and activism that overcomes its own limits, that experiments with itself and the world.

Doubtless this spells more self-initiated rehabs and rebuilding of peripheral *banlieues*, of rundown HLMs and *grands ensembles*, as well as more occupations of vacant buildings and lots the world over, those foreclosed and abandoned speculative properties, unused patches of land awaiting private plunder; even whole strip malls in the United States lie empty, over-built and under-used. That's a lot of steady work for *sans-culottes* to wage war on two flanks, on those inner and outer flanks that Hazan identifies: on the one hand, occupy these vacant spaces, squat them and take them back, rebuild them in a new communal image, reinventing them as spaces in which people can encounter one another and new affinities can be forged; there, small-scale retailing might flourish within over-accumulated and devalued giant retailing. These devalued spaces can revalorize as new Main Streets on the edge, new centers of urban life with green space, with organic small-holdings, with social housing, self-organized by people for people rather than for profit. Creative destruction, at last, might allow for non-patented creativity.

On the other hand, the outer propulsion of the insurrection must continue to occupy the spaces of the 1 percent, of our financial and corporate aristocracy, fighting the banks, financial institutions and corporations who spearhead neo-Haussmannization, protest and denounce them on their own turf, downtown, at the centers of their wealth and power, making a racket while liberating the spaces these shysters have foreclosed, abandoned and repelled. It's not so farfetched to call this global ruling class an "aristocracy" because they have much in common with the parasitic elites of yesteryear. For one thing, their profits and capital accumulation have arisen from a marked penchant for *dispossession*; they've shown zilch commitment to investing in living labor in actual production.

Much wealth comes from titles to rent, resultant of land monopolization and real estate speculation, and from interest accruing from financial assets, many of which are purely fictitious and extortionately make-believe, including make-believe service charges and transaction fees incurred on borrowers. (People seem to pay up these make-believe fees, come what may, and make them hard-to-believe fees instead, the awful truth of parasitic capitalism.) Unsurprisingly, profits have little to do with corporations investing in salaried workers and making quality products at lower prices than their competitors, doing all the things "good" capitalists are supposed to do. Invariably, it's more to do with scrounging corporate welfare, tax avoidance and monopolization, with destroying competition within a given field. The enormous growth in wealth means more and more redundant workers; living labor is a species en route to extinction, thus *sans-culottes*—who're often *sans papiers* as well as *sans travail*.

* * *

Hazan's great inspiration for insurrection is the "June Days" of 1848, more so than the Commune itself, because the latter, says Hazan in his foreword to Lissagaray's *History of the Paris Commune*, started off as "a patriotic upsurge, a gesture of national pride, before being a revolutionary social movement."[5] The June Days of 1848 were a truly authentic insurrection of the *sans-culottes*, one that can set the terms for *l'insurrection qui vient* (or *qui viendrait*) in our day. Even the voice of Order, the conservative-liberal commentator Alexis de Tocqueville, marveled in his *Recollections* (staple reading for Guy Debord) at those June Days, "the greatest and strangest insurrection that had ever taken place in our history." Tocqueville could almost be describing Occupy, circa September 2011: "the greatest [insurrection] because insurgents were fighting without a battle cry, leaders, or flag, and yet they showed wonderful powers of coordination."[6] Yet if Tocqueville is brilliant and surprisingly generous at analyzing what insurgents did between February and June 1848, he's also damning about what they failed to do after assuming power, and after *La Garde mobile* marched into town. (The CRS and the privatized security force of the RATP are *La Garde mobile*'s latter-day reincarnations.)

5. Hazan, "Foreword to 2012 Edition," in Prosper-Olivier Lissagaray's *History of the Paris Commune*, Verso, London, 2012.
6. Alexis de Tocqueville, *Recollections*, Anchor Books, New York, 1971, p. 169.

The June Days were a revolt of the "unknown," initiated by an anonymous rank-and-file, by a nobody urban proletariat, ordinary men and women "who gave events their color and explain in part why they're now forgotten." 1848 is the most important insurrection in working-class history, says Hazan, because it "marked the severing of an implicit pact, or, if you like, the end of an illusion: that the people and the bourgeoisie, hand-in-hand, were going to finish what they'd started in the Revolution [of 1789]."[7] Today, we've seen another illusion put to an end, punctured, a rupturing with our own post-war consensus (and dissensus): that of paternal capitalism giving ordinary people a break, of a bourgeoisie and workers establishing a just social contract together. All bets are now summarily off. What we've seen instead is the end of an era of expectations: expectations of steady jobs, with decent pay, with benefits, with security and pensions; the whole bit.

Experiments in living today necessarily mean having no expectations in life, except those you create yourself, invent yourself, including the insurrection—an insurrection in which economic self-empowerment encounters political collective-empowerment; the favelas as well as financial districts, *banlieues* as well as bidonvilles, the malls as well as Main Streets would all get occupied then, democratized by an inexorable and an insatiable *swarming*, by a sheer numbers-game asserting itself as a political subjects-game. At that point, the barricades wouldn't so much go up in the center of the city (*à la* Commune) as those barricades that separate centers from peripheries would get torn down, removed within the tissuing of global urban space. Such is my wish-image for the coming insurrection, for the new civil war unfolding across the planet, for the new urban question, from below, answered from below, answerable to the below. For the moment, Hazan knows, just as I know—just as Tocqueville knew back in 1848—that the fighting has stopped, even if it is due to start again any day soon. "The insurrection was everywhere contained," says Tocqueville, "but nowhere tamed."[8]

7. Hazan, *Paris sous tension*, p. 64.
8. Tocqueville, *Recollections*, p. 192.

4

Strategic Embellishment and Urban Civil War

Of all of politics I understand only one thing: the revolt.

—Gustave Flaubert cited in Benjamin's "The Paris of the Second Empire in Baudelaire"

No matter how many times you read Walter Benjamin's musings on Paris they never disappoint. They never sound worn; there are always new nuggets buried within, lurking between the lines, little sparkling gems you never expected to find, nor saw upon your first reading. There is always something, too, that speaks as much about our century as the fabled nineteenth, over which Paris, Benjamin said, majestically presided. He spent hours upon hours—years and years in fact—scribbling away under "the painted sky of summer," beneath the huge ceiling mural of Paris's *Bibliothèque Nationale de France* (BNF), amassing piles of notes (some still apparently lying unpublished, gathering dust in BNF's vaults) on the arcades project that so mesmerized him, on Fourier and Marx, on Baudelaire and Blanqui, on Haussmann and insurrection. Those latter two themes—Haussmannization and insurrection—have piqued my interest again recently, helped me frame and reframe my thinking about what I've been calling here "the new urban question."

"Speculation on the stock-exchange," says Benjamin, commenting on "Haussmann or the Barricades," "pushed into the background the forms of gambling that had come down from feudal society."[1]

1. Walter Benjamin, "Haussmann or the Barricades," in Benjamin, *Charles Baudelaire: A Lyric Poet in the Era of High Capitalism*, Verso, London, 1983, p. 174.

Gambling transformed time, he says, into a heady narcotic, into an orgy of speculation over space, seemingly addictive for the wealthy and indispensable for the fraudulent. (The two, unsurprisingly, fed off one another then and still do.) Finance capital began to make its sleazy *entrée* into the urban experience; beforehand the urban was simply the backdrop of a great capitalist drama unfolding around the time Marx wrote the *Manifesto*. It was simply the seat of the stock market; suddenly, though, the urban itself became a stock market, another asset. Now wheeling and dealing became wheeling and dealing in urban space, state-sponsored real estate promotion, investing in configuring new space and in expropriating old space. The devil's bargain between politics and economics underwent its modern consecration.

Benjamin underscores two principal characteristics of Louis-Bonaparte's master-builder Baron Haussmann—who, remember, prided himself on his self-anointed nickname: *l'artiste démolisseur* ["demolition artist"].[2] (The title "Baron" was actually a purely egotistical creation as well, having no official credence.) Haussmann's first characteristic was an immense hatred of the masses, of the poor, of rootless homeless populations, the wretched and ragged victims of his giant wreckers-ball, displaced denizens that are immortalized in Charles Baudelaire's "Eyes of the Poor" *Paris Spleen* poem. Benjamin recalls a speech Haussmann made in 1864 at the National Assembly, fulminating about the stepchildren his grand works had actively created. "This population kept increasing as a result of his works," Benjamin says. "The increase in rents drove the proletariat into the suburbs." Central Paris thereby lost its "popular" base, "lost its characteristic physiognomy." Typical of so many tyrant-visionaries (like Robert Moses, who admired his gallic antecedent), Haussmann was a bundle of contradictions: publicly-minded (his underground sewers and macadamized boulevards replaced shitty overground drains and boggy lanes), yet scornful of real people; a lover of Paris, "the city of all Frenchmen," yet suspicious of democratic elections and progressive taxation. Haussmann saw it all as his God-given duty, his natural right "to expropriate for the cause of public utility."

2. Benjamin, *Charles Baudelaire*, p. 174.

Yet, for Benjamin, there was something else behind Haussmann's works, a second, perhaps more important theme: "the securing of the city against civil war," a desperate desire to prevent the barricades going up across the city's streets. A red fear. The breadth of those new boulevards would, it was thought, make future barricade building trickier, a more onerous and protracted ordeal in the heat of any revolt. Besides, "the new streets," says Benjamin, "were to provide the shortest route between the barracks and the working-class areas." Hence the forces of order could more quickly mobilize themselves, more rapidly crush a popular insurrection. Urban space was concurrently profitable and pragmatic, aesthetically edifying yet militarily convenient; "strategic embellishment," Benjamin labels it, a vocation eagerly practiced to this very day, though with new twists and turns.[3]

* * *

The new twists and turns are the scale of this dialectic, the depth and breadth of the twin forces of strategic embellishment and insurrection. This dialectic is *immanent* in the our current urban-global condition, and respective antagonists feed off one another in dramatic ways. They are both immanent within the upheaval of our neoliberal market economy, just as Marx said that a relative surplus population was immanent in the accumulation of capital; and therein, borrowing Benjamin's valedictory words, "we can begin to recognize the monuments of the bourgeoisie as ruins even before they have crumbled." As I've said, we can pinpoint Haussmann-like acts in every city across the globe, North and South, East and West; but it's vital to see all this as a process that engineers planetary urban space. We need, in other words, to open out our vista, to see the global urban wood rather than just the city trees, to see an individual despotic program as a generalized class imperative, as a process of neo-Haussmannization, as something consciously planned as well as unconsciously initiated, pretty much everywhere.

3. Benjamin, *Charles Baudelaire*, p. 175.

Our planetary urban fabric—the terrestrial texturing of our urban universe—is woven by a ruling class that sees cities as purely speculative entities, as sites for gentrifying schemes and upscale redevelopments, as machines for making clean, quick money in, and for dispossessing erstwhile public goods. Cities therein are microcosmic parasitic entities embedded in a macrocosmic urban system, discrete atoms with their own inner laws of quantum gravity, responsive to a general theory of global relativity. Splitting city molecules reveal elemental charges within: let's call them "centers" and "peripheries," complementarities of attraction and repulsion, of speculative particles and insurrectional waves. Is there a master-builder therein, some great God presiding over these heavenly bodies, a living Baron Haussmann? Yes and No.

Yes, because there are certainly prime movers in making deals, actual class embodiments of finance capital and speculative real estate interests, real lenders and borrows, actual developers and builders, breathing architects and administrators, some of whom are moguls who mobilize their might like the Baron of old; all, too, have their own local flavoring and place-specific ways of doing things, culturally conditioned dependent on where you are, and, moreover, on what you can get away with. Degrees of maneuverability and financial shenanigans are of course negatively correlated to degrees of regulation, whether the latter exists or doesn't.

In another sense, although there are complicit individuals, both in public and private office, with varying degrees of competence, who may even be cognizant of one another, in explicit cahoots with one another, it'd be mistaken to see it all as one giant conspiracy—a "Great Game," as Kipling quipped of English imperialism in India—as a single coordinated global conspiracy undertaken by an omnipotent ruling class. Indeed, that would attribute too much to this aristocratic elite, over-estimate their sway over the entirety of urban space. That's why we'd also say "no" to the above question about God-like master builders.[4]

4. Ibsen's play *The Master-Builder* [1892] points to the frailty of the apparently successful builder's ego, the rationalization that their particular gifts are gifts from God. Solness, Ibsen's eponymous master-builder, has amassed

But what's abundantly clear, as Haussmann knew, is that to peripheralize people en masse necessitates the insulation of centers. Insulation means controlling borders, patrolling risk, damming leakiness, keeping people out as well as in; "control," the Invisible Committee say in *The Coming Insurrection*, "has a wonderful way of integrating itself into the commodity landscape, showing its authoritarian face to anyone who wants to see it. It's an age of fusions, of muzak, telescopic police batons and cotton candy. Equal parts police surveillance and enchantment!"[5] That's the nub of neo-Haussmannization, its law of social physics. Thus aristocrats in our age of Enlightenment acknowledge their fear of the *sans-culottes* they help create, the citizens they disenfranchise, the deracinated they banish to the global *banlieues*.

Thus the civil war is everyday, is about strategic security in the face of economic volatility; and the stakes have ratcheted up since 9/11. In fact, 9/11 set the terms of a whole new set of odds about what is now permissible. The "war on terrorism" gets reenacted on the everyday civilian urban street, where "low intensity conflicts" justify paramilitary policing and counter-insurgency tactics—just in case. (For a graphic survey, we need look no further than Steve Graham's brilliant exposé, *Cities Under Siege*.[6] "The war on terror operations in London," says Graham, "efforts to securitize and militarize cities during G-20 summits and other mega-events, the counter-drug and counter-terror efforts in the favelas of Rio ... link very closely to the full-scale counterinsurgency warfare and colonial control operations in places like Baghdad or the West Bank.")

---

considerable fame and fortune from his fortunate series of construction exploits. Yet it's never enough; his paranoia abounds, this mania to uphold supernatural powers, including sexual powers. Ibsen starkly emphasizes Solness's fantasies as indicators of looming madness. Such, it seems, is the master-builder's lot. The other thing that strikes, when one looks at the operation of today's most powerful financial institutions, like banks, who are often at the fore of the construction business, is a ubiquitous and consistent managerial incompetence.

5. The Invisible Committee, *The Coming Insurrection*, Semiotext(e), Los Angeles, CA, 2009, p. 53.
6. Stephen Graham, *Cities Under Siege: The New Military Urbanism*, Verso, London, 2010.

The fragmented shards of global neo-Haussmannization are likewise reassembled as a singular narrative in Eric Hazan's *Chronique de la guerre civile*: "nonstop wail of police sirens on the boulevard Barbès, the whistling of F16s high in the sky over Palestine, rumbling tanks rattling the earth in Grozny and Tikrit, armored bulldozers crushing houses in Rafah, bombs exploding over Baghdad and on buses in Jerusalem, barking attack dogs accompanying security forces on the Paris metro"—all provide testimony of a business-as-usual battle scene in an ongoing global urban civil war. In fact, paramilitary policing in Palestine, says Hazan, serves as something of a model everywhere for "the war of the *banlieue*."[7] Jerusalem isn't any further from Ramallah than Drancy is from Notre-Dame; yet it's a war in the periphery that's rendered invisible from the standpoint of the center. ("In Tel-Aviv, you can live as peacefully as in Vésinet or in Deauville.") And behind all the din and shocks, the bombs and barking, global centers experiment with new depersonalized high-technology, unleashing democracy at 30,000 ft, modern warfare orchestrated on a computer keyboard. (High-tech Israelis are closely linked with American research institutes and with the military-industrial complex; arms trade and patents are worth billions of dollars. "The military and the monetary get together when it's necessary," rapped the late Gil Scott-Heron; he left out the academy, or "the academary," which goes together with the military and the monetary when it's necessary.)

* * *

A force is a push or pull exerted upon an object resultant from its interaction with another object. Centers and peripheries emanate from such interaction, from such *contact* interaction, from a Newtonian Third Law of Motion: for every action there is an equal and opposite reaction. We can name that oppositional reaction *insurrection*, even if, in the Third Law of Newtonian Social and Political Motion, that reaction is opposite but never equal; it is a

7. Eric Hazan, *Chronique de la guerre civile*, Éditions la fabrique, Paris, 2003, p. 32.

minority reaction despite being voiced by a majority; it is a reaction that creates its own action, or, as *The Coming Insurrection* suggests, its own *resonance*. Insurrection resonates from the impact of the shock waves summoned up by bombs and banishment, all of which unleash reactive and active waves of friction and opposition, alternative vibrations that spread from the *banlieues*, that ripple through the periphery and seep into the center.

If there are twin powers of insurrection, one internal, another external, an outer propulsive energy, then it's the latter which might hold the key in any battle to come, in any global intifada. And here it's not so much a solidarity between Palestinian kids lobbing rocks and *casseurs* in Seine-Saint-Denis, between jobless Spaniards and Greeks taking over Madrid's Puerta del Sol and Athen's Syntagma Square, between school kids in Chile and looters in Croydon, nor even between the Occupy movement in the U.S. and its sister cells across the globe; it's more that each of these groups somehow see themselves in different camps of the *same* civil war, fighting as territorial foot soldiers, as relative surplus populations sharing a common language and, significantly, a common enemy.

The war of the *banlieue* is a special kind of war, the scene of military maneuvering different from warfare of old, staged on an open battlefield. This war no longer comprises grandiose campaigns by troops but is rather a micro-everydayness of peacetime intervention, a dogged affair in which the police and the paramilitary play interchangeable roles, indiscernible roles. Maintaining order and destabilizing order require new urban tactics, different from past warfare and previous insurrections. The terrain of the civil war is now at once more claustrophobic and more fluid, more intensive as well as more extensive. The urban needs to be theorized as a tissue with capillaries and arteries through which blood and energy circulate to nourish this tissue, to keep its cells alive, or sometimes to leave them partly dead from under-nutrition or blockage. This understanding lets us see the urban's complex circuit card, its networked patterning, its mosaic and fractal form, stitched together with pieces of loose fabric; an organism massively complex yet strikingly vulnerable.

Insurrectional forces must enter into its flow, into the capillaries and arteries of urban power and wealth, enter into its global network to interrupt that circulation and reproduction of capital, to unwind its variable webbing and fixed infrastructure, to occupy its nodes at the most powerful points, while, Leninist-style, decoupling the system's weakest links. In a way, given the global interconnectivity of everything, this can be done almost anywhere, accepting there are nodes that assume relative priority in the system's overall functioning. Just as cybernetic information can be hacked, so too can acts of subversion interrupt and hack flows of money, distribution of goods, movements of transport. The system can be stymied as a circulatory process, as a process that needs to reproduce itself, through the progressive production of apoplexy. We've seen symbolic stymying, like outside Wall Street or St. Paul's Cathedral, yet we've also seen real apoplexy, when, in December 2011, Occupy Oakland took over the U.S.'s fifth-largest port, "Wall Street on the waterfront," crippling operating revenues that amount to a hefty annual $27 billion, striking aristocrats hard where it hurts them most: in their pockets, right on the ground.

Perhaps sabotage is a valid retribution for the incivilities that reign in our streets? "The police are not invincible in the streets," the Invisible Committee write, "they simply have the means to organize, train, and continually test new weapons. Our weapons, on the other hand, are always rudimentary, cobbled together, and often improvised on the spot."[8] The power of surprise, of secret organization, of rebelling, of demonstrating and plotting covertly, of striking invisibly, and in multiple sites at once, is the key element in confronting a power whose firepower is vastly superior. Once, in the past, sabotaging and thwarting work, slowing down the speed of work, breaking up the machines and working-to-rule comprised a valid modus operandi, an effective weapon for hindering production and lock-jamming the economy; now, the space of twenty-first-century urban circulation, of the ceaseless and often mindless current of commodities and people, of information and energy, of cars and communication, becomes the broadened dimension of the "whole social factory" to which the principle of sabotage can be applied.

8. The Invisible Committee, *The Coming Insurrection*, pp. 115–16.

Thus "jam everything" becomes a reflex principle of critical negativity, of Bartlebyism brought back to radical life, of Newton's Third Law of Political Motion. Ironically, the more the economy has rendered itself virtual, and the more "delocalized," "dematerialized" and "just-in-time" is its infrastructural base, the easier it is to take down locally, to create apoplexy, to redirect and reappropriate. Several years ago, insurrections in France against CPE bill (*contrat première embauche*), the first of a series of state laws to make job contracts for young people more insecure, "did not hesitate to block train stations, ring roads, factories, highways, supermarkets and even airports." In Rennes, the Invisible Committee recall, "only three hundred people were needed to shut down the main access road to the town for hours and cause a 40-kilometer long traffic jam."[9] Blanqui, too, that professional insurrectionist, the shady conspiratorial figure who so fascinated Benjamin (and Baudelaire), likewise recognized how urban space isn't simply the theater of confrontation; it's also the means and stake in an insurrection, the battleground of a guerrilla warfare that builds barricades and gun turrets, that occupies buildings and strategic spaces, that employs the methodology of moving through walls.

But barricades today aren't there simply to defend inwardly. They need to be flexible and portable, and outward looking. They need to move between nodes to disrupt and block, as well as foster new life within. They need to be mobilized to tear down other barricades that keep people apart, that trap people in, that peripheralize. Those latter sort of barricades are walls of fear that need smashing down like the veritable storming of the Bastille, so that new spaces of encounter can be formed—new agoras for assemblies of the people, for peoples' Assembly.

Benjamin was mesmerized by the spirit of Blanqui haunting Haussmann's boulevards, Blanqui the antidote to Haussmannization, Blanqui the live fuse for igniting civil war, for catalyzing insurrectional eruption. And although Blanqui's secret cells of revolutionary agents—those hardened, fully-committed professional conspirators—had an inherent mistrust of the masses, Benjamin

9. The Invisible Committee, *The Coming Insurrection*, p. 125.

nonetheless saw in them a capacity to organize and propagandize, to spread the insurrectional word, to figure out a plan and give that plan definition and purpose. They could even help guide an activism that seizes territories and schemes mass desertion; that could, in our day, reinvent a neo-Blanquism (neo-Jacobinism?) to confront intensifying neo-Haussmannization, an opposite and almost equal reaction. Indeed, perhaps the thing that most fascinated Benjamin was Blanqui's notion of "eternal recurrence," that stuff comes around full circle, including revolutions, that democratic passions don't disappear: they crop up again and again in new forms and in different guises, with new tricks and covert tactics, with new participants whose prescient ability is to reimagine the dominant order as ruins even before it has crumbled.

5

Sentimental Urban Education

> Generations of people are like leaves. The wind casts leaves to the ground, but the fertile forest brings forth others, and spring comes around again.
>
> —Homer, *The Iliad*

For a long while I've been fascinated by another arch-conspirator, the Situationist "guru" Guy Debord, who likewise reimagined the ruins of the dominant order before it had crumbled. If anything, I've probably been a little too fascinated by Debord for my own good, since his strange grip on my thinking about the world in part led me to quit my job as a paid-up academic, throwing in my lot with freelance wandering and writing. I'd only ever encountered Debord on the page, and on film, never in person. But I did meet his widow once, Alice Becker-Ho, in Champot Haut, a hamlet in the Haute-Loire, inside the portcullis of a house where Debord had shot himself in the heart. We'd sat on the edge of the lawn in the shade during a heatwave, a *canicule*, around a table with a green tablecloth. I'd told her about my book project on her late husband, which I was then calling *Land of Storms*, a book that never materialized as such. "It's here," she'd said, raising her hand to the sky, acknowledging the Champot of Debord's *Panégyrique*, his slim autobiography from 1989:

> They approached noiselessly at first, announced by a brief passage of a wind that slithered through the grass or by a series of sudden flashes on the horizon; then thunder and lightening unleashed, and we were bombarded for a long time, and from every direction, as if in a fortress under siege. One time, at night, I saw lightening strike near me, outside: you could not even see where it had struck; the whole landscape was equally illuminated for a startling instant.

> Nothing in art seemed to give me this impression of an irrevocable brilliance, except for the prose that Lautréamont employed in the programmatic exposition that he called *Poésies*.[1]

Debord himself was something of a prophet of storms and violent winds: he'd lived through a lot of them, and conjured up a few more in his own vivid imagination. "All my life," he began *Panégyrique*, "I have seen only troubled times, extreme divisions in society, and immense destruction; I have taken part in these troubles." I remember telling Alice about the two metaphors I wanted to deploy in my book: one about the wall, *à la* Clausewitz, as a defense against an exterior menace, against spectacular intrusion, a buttress capable of resisting attack, a high wall I could glimpse right in front of me as we spoke; the other, the notion of the Seine, of a river always flowing, constantly moving, like a vagabond traveler, like a discoverer of liberty through motion, always dodging an enemy, shrugging off the overbearing weight of the dominant order. Then I told her that within these two metaphors, I wanted to bring to bear Pierre Mac Orlan's idea, from his *Petit manuel du parfait aventurier*, of the passive and active adventurer. Thus, within the walls of their defense, the passive adventurer re-imagines and recreates the world as dream, in the domain of language and poetry, or as a lost twilight world of yesterday; the active adventurer, meantime, is a peripatetic voyager who actually does travel from place to place, who seeks out novelty beyond the page, and really does try to lose and find themselves. I tell Madame Debord that I picture Monsieur Debord's resistance in this dual light. "Ah yes, Guy loved that Mac Orlan book," she said. "He'd read it many times over, knew it well. He adored Pierre Mac Orlan."

* * *

Petit manuel du parfait aventurier is an intriguing text hailing from 1920. Within the space of 60 or so tight leaves, in his *little manual for the perfect adventurer*, French novelist Pierre Mac Orlan presents some compelling, if pretty offbeat, notions about adventure: "It's

1. Guy Debord, *Panégyrique*, Verso, London, 1989, pp. 48–9.

necessary to establish, as a law," Mac Orlan says, "that adventure doesn't exist."[2] Adventure is more about *fantastique social*, he says, and Mac Orlan's novels, like his life, brim with just that. The *fantastique social* is a sensibility neither supernatural nor paranormal, but profoundly everyday, reserved for back streets and damaged people, for twilight nooks and crannies, for shadowy bars and taverns, often adjacent to water, animated by liquor and dramatized by departure—departures never made. One glimpses the urban fantastic for a thrilling instant, taps its hidden recesses by tapping the idiosyncrasies of the imagination. "To give an explanation to the fantastic," says Mac Orlan, "is a difficult thing. All explanations of the fantastic are, besides, arbitrary. The fantastic, like adventure, only exists in the imagination of those who search for it. One reaches, by chance, the goal of adventure. Try as one does to penetrate its aura, the mysterious elements that populate it disappear."[3]

Mac Orlan reckons there are two types of adventurer. On the one hand, we have those daring men of action (they're usually men)—people who run off to join the Foreign Legion, who set sail with the navy, climb mountains, go up in hot air balloons, do bungee jumping. These "active adventurers" explore to forget, to seek fortune, to find distraction, let testosterone flow; they desperately "need to conquer," Mac Orlan says. For the active adventurer, "certain traits are essential: the total absence of imagination and feeling. They don't fear death because they can't explain it; but they fear those who are clearly stronger than them."[4]

Contrast that with "passive adventurers." They, on the other hand, are more fastidious, more cerebral, more studious and solitary explorers, reading a lot and dreaming often, taking to the pen as much as the high sea. Their voyages are commonplace, more carefully chosen: cities and cabarets, burlesque and books, wine and song, love and hate, intimacy and death. They never learnt to swim but can probably play the accordion and know, by heart, every sailor shanty.

2. Pierre Mac Orlan, *Petit manuel du parfait aventurier*, Mercure de France, Paris, 1994, p. 15.
3. Mac Orlan, *Petit manuel du parfait aventurier*, p. 15.
4. Mac Orlan, *Petit manuel du parfait aventurier*, p. 22.

Passive adventuring is an art form, says Mac Orlan, "a question of intellectual gymnastics, understanding everyday exercises and practicing the methodology of the imagination."[5]

The conflicting impulse of passive and active adventuring underwrites the whole of Mac Orlan's oeuvre, and is brilliantly played out in *Villes*, his charming memoir from 1929. A typical mixture of rhetoric and reality, *Villes* evokes wanderings and seaports, grubby back streets and shady, twilight characters, all of which hark back to another age, to a sentimental education seldom found on any latter-day urban curriculum. Nocturnal street corners wend and weft their way through *Villes*; as we leaf through its time-served pages, beat-up personalities and nettle-ridden paving stones invade our living rooms and possess our minds. Suddenly, somehow, we find ourselves foisted backwards to fin-de-siècle Montmartre, outside the Lapin Agile tavern, sauntering along the rue Saint-Vincent in summertime, or loitering in winter at the Place du Tertre, feeling its icy chill penetrate our threadbare overcoat. In Mac Orlan's Montmartre, "dance halls and the specious appearance of an ancient little village distill into a subtle poison of laziness and insomnia."[6]

Villes also invites us to smell the sea, at Brest, to stroll down rue de Siam, "a river whose waters are richly populated and whose catch is always fruitful." In Brest, "under a sky of prehistoric gray," we can hear foghorns and the clatter of clogs and can push open the shutters of bars that want to surrender themselves to the sea. "One doesn't come to Brest," says Mac Orlan, "to enjoy life, to flaunt an elegant dress, or to recuperate in the sun; other reasons, those the sea doesn't ignore, lead men and women toward this city without liners or departures. For here adventure wafts like a bellowing salty breeze."[7] Pungent adventures also waft across the Channel in *Villes*, to London's Commercial Road, where, with Mac Orlan, we can reenact scenes from Dr. Jekyll and Mr. Hyde, and where, "at midnight, a cold and luminous sadness seizes you by the shoulders or touches you high on the arms like a police baton." "In this long and naked street,

---

5. Mac Orlan, *Petit manuel du parfait aventurier*, p. 28.
6. Pierre Mac Orlan, *Villes*, Gallimard, Paris, 1924, p. 64.
7. Mac Orlan, *Villes*, p. 133.

permeated with a vague odor of opium and gin, under dazzling and sterile lamplight, there is," Mac Orlan says, "just me and my shadow."[8] In *Villes*, we wander melancholically a step behind Mac Orlan's shadowy presence, a journey an aging Guy Debord made many times over, especially in post-1968 exile, entering Mac Orlan's enchanting urban labyrinth himself, with its cascading array of back-alleys and mangled memories, and wounded warriors and warped waysides.

* * *

Mac Orlan's and Debord's vagabond peregrinations are 50 years apart; yet both follow a well-trodden path staked out by François Villon, the medieval poet and *mauvais garçon*, the bad boy who kept bad company. Villon wrote intensely personal and lyrical poetry, like his masterpiece *The Testament* [1462], together with wonderfully ribald verses in slang that Mac Orlan and Debord fondly cite in their books. Villon adopts the argot of the *Coquillards*, an organized criminal underworld with their own secret language, a tongue no outsider can decipher. The poet had loose *Coquillard* connections; his friend, Régnier de Montigny, petty hood, cop-beater and kleptomaniac, a prototypical Jean Genet character, was a *Coquillard*, as was Colin de Cayeux, one of Villon's companions in the notorious College of Navarre robbery, when one Christmas night they climbed over a high wall, picked the lock of a safe, and made off with the school's booty. "Keep changing outfits," Villon preaches, "and ducking into churches; / take off, make sure your / clothes don't trip you up. / To show the others / they strung up Montigny; / he babbled to the crowd a while, / and then the hangman snapped his neck . . . Prince of jerks who stick around, / hit the open road, move on, / and always keep your eyes peeled / for the hangman's filthy paws."[9] The warnings are instructive for modern readers and radicals.

"The Montmartre of my twenties," Mac Orlan says, "was clearly inspired by France's finest popular poet. His silhouette wandered

8. Mac Orlan, *Villes*, pp. 176–7.
9. François Villon, *The Complete Works of François Villon*, Bantam Books, New York, 1960, p. 173.

along the walls of the rue des Saules and in front of the mass grave of Saint Vincent, disturbed by the heckles of the young Mademoiselles sat at the Lapin Agile's grand table . . . His shadow wandered in the twilight between the trees of the Place du Tertre, near the old kiosk, now long gone, where police bobbies stood watch by night."[10] Villon's spirit is there with young Mac Orlan's velvet underground of painters and poets (like Picasso and Apollinaire), of geniuses and deadbeats who haunted lower and upper Montmartre, yearning for a little bread, some love, and a warm bed. Adventures here were full of risky business and barroom brawls where nobody really gets hurt and where protagonists have nothing to fear but themselves. "Villon played with loaded dice," says Mac Orlan, "in the company of Régnier de Montigny. We had all known in our life a Régnier de Montigny for dealing the cards. But the *Coquillards* of the rue Cortot or the rue des Saules knew how to hang themselves on the gallows of fortune without the intervention of the executioner."[11]

"We had several points of resemblance," Debord says in *Panégyrique*, "with those other devotees of the dangerous life who had spent their time, exactly five hundred years before us, in the same city and on the same side of the river . . . There had been that noble man among my friends who was the complete equal of Régnier de Montigny, as well as many other rebels destined for bad ends; and there were the pleasures and splendor of those lost young hoodlum girls [*voyelles*] who kept us such good company in our dives and couldn't have been that different from the girls the others had known under the names of Marion l'Idole or Catherine, Biétrix and Bellet."[12] Throughout the 1950s and 1960s, Debord and his band of *Coquillards*—"demolition experts," he likened them (p. 16), upending Haussmann—inhabited their own little patch, their own "zone of perdition" where, he says, "his youth went as if to achieve its education" and where adventures always seemed closer to home, imaginative leaps of the mind and spirit, intellectual and political acts of defiance and debauchery.

10. Pierre Mac Orlan, "Montmartre," in *Oeuvres complètes de Pierre Mac Orlan*, Gilbert Sigaux, Genève, 1969, p. 21.
11. Mac Orlan, "Montmartre," p. 85.
12. Debord, *Panégyrique*, p. 26.

Indeed, Debord admits: "I haven't had the need to travel very far . . . Most of the time I lived in Paris, exactly in the triangle defined by the intersections of the rue Saint-Jacques and the rue Royer-Colland, rue Saint Martin and rue Greneta, and the rue du Bac and rue de Commailles."[13] A smallish area, accessible on foot, spanning both sides of the Seine, between Les Halles and the Pantheon, in the 3rd and 5th arrondissements; there, says Debord, he spent his days and nights, and would never have left if the life he'd led there hadn't been completely destroyed.

It was a milieu of "dangerous classes," of malcontents and poor engaged in perilous pursuits. Everybody knew how to live off the land—the urban land. They were lost prophets of an almost bygone age now, an age of innocence and naiveté, of espresso and wine and mad, raving ideals. They wandered in the night and were consumed by fire. Everybody around Debord was young and fanatical, talked about philosophy, art, film, politics, and drank a lot, usually in cheap cafés and bars, sometimes with poor students in the Latin Quarter, other times with the lumpenproletariat of the Marais. This was the light that shone so intensely for Debord, radiant against a backdrop of Art Blakey's "Whisper Not." An infamous Debordian hole-in-the-wall where he and others hung out and drank was Chez Moineau's on the rue du Four. Close to the fashionable existentialist world of "Café de Flore" and "Les Deux Magots," it was a universe away in terms of clientele. Under Debord's poor cloak was an already legendary drinker. He was a regular at Chez Moineau's, whose mainstay wasn't bourgeois highbrow types, like Sartre and de Beauvoir, but hoods and gangsters, prostitutes and pimps, dropouts and runaways, petty criminals and time-served boozers, latter-day accomplices of François Villon, misfit characters from the pages of Céline, Mac Orlan and Genet. This *demi-monde* was his perpetual source of play and adventure. "Paris then," says Debord, "never slept, and permitted you to debauch and change neighborhoods three times each night. Its inhabitants hadn't yet been driven away and dispersed."[14]

---

13. Debord, *Panégyrique*, p. 43.
14. Guy Debord, "Girum Imus Nocte Consumimur Igni," in *Oeuvres cinématographique complètes de Guy Debord*, Gallimard, Paris, 1994, p. 223.

* * *

The bulldozers and the wrecker's ball never made it to the Latin Quarter, not since Haussmann's own day anyway; but tourist cafés, wine bars and restaurants, as well as the antique stores and chic boutiques, carried out under neo-Haussmannization, have just as effectively seen off the neighborhood. Montparnasse Tower, Paris's first skyscraper, gave it the added finger. Unsurprisingly, Moineau's is a distant memory. Dodging traffic across the Boulevard Saint-Germain, and journeying on to rue du Four, offers little novelty for the present-day wanderer, for any intrepid urbanist intent on serendipity, on retracing *les pas perdus*. This is where Debord found and lost his youth, where "we no more than other men could stay sober on this watch." But it's a watch that has now undergone solid *embourgeoisement*. Nobody would suspect number 22's past life either, that tiny bar whose clientele dreamt about changing the world, of setting it ablaze only to give it more light and warmth. These days, Chez Moineau's takes on a perverse New Age twist, a store selling all sorts of scented wares and herbs for yuppies and preppies, for people who don't know what to spend their surplus cash on.

Everywhere around rue du Four and rue de Buci is beautiful: the buildings are beautiful, the people are beautiful, the streets are clean and nice, and central Paris looks just as amazingly alluring. But the romance has long gone: the place no longer lives, no longer breathes, palpitates, no longer has intrigue or mystery. The landscape is flat, empty, predictable: the future is closed, sealed by market forces; the center is now a spectacular showcase, a polished ornament: reel life has vanquished real life. "Between the rue du Four and the rue de Buci," says Debord in *Panégyrique*, "where our youth so completely went astray as a few glasses were drunk, one could feel certain that we would never do any better."[15] But he could do better than what we have here: "There is no greater folly than the present organization of life." Those "bards of conditioning," Debord knew, had *assassinated* Paris, making a killing in the process. The city had died in his arms, in her prime, from a "fatal illness," a

15. Debord, *Panégyrique*, p. 38.

fatal illness "carrying off all the major cities, and this illness is itself only one of the numerous symptoms of the material decadence of a society. But Paris had more to lose than any other. It was great good fortune to have been young in this town when, for the last time, it shone with so intense a fire."

Debord adored Paris: it was his stomping ground, his laboratory. He bore the burden of its travails, taking them very personally, very politically. He was what Antonio Gramsci would have labeled an "organic intellectual": he belonged to a place and to a people, and he felt their "elemental passions." And yet, more and more, this belonging and Debord's kind were being threatened, were being displaced, torn down and torn apart, as neighborhoods began to get readjusted and reordered. Henri Lefebvre remembered his friendship with Debord lasting from about 1957 to 1962. The sociology professor was teaching Marxism at Strasbourg then, and there, around 1958, he'd met and taught other younger Situationists. Lefebvre lived in Paris near to Debord and Michéle Bernstein, and remembered them inhabiting "a kind of studio on rue Saint Martin, in a dark room, no lights at all." It was "a miserable place, but at the same time a place where there was a great deal of strength and radiance in the thinking and the research."[16]

Parisian rents were bearable back then; cheap thrills were still to be had, cold-water affordability was possible. Debord lived only a stone's throw away from Les Halles, from the old fruit and vegetable market halls, destined to be demolished in 1971, to make way for the RER rapid regional commuter train. (The Pompidou Center, completed six years later, would seal the neighborhood's fate.) Before that, Les Halles had been a sprawling, delirious, humdrum world, intensely alive, bawdy and beautiful, an urban paradise for Debord. When Baudelaire wrote in his poem "Le Voyage," "To plunge into the abyss . . . And find in depths of the unknown the new," it might have been old Les Halles he was describing. But by the mid-1970s that world was nigh gone, assassinated in the name of economic progress

16. Henri Lefebvre, "Interview: Henri Lefebvre and the Situationists International," *October* (Winter 1997), Number 97, p. 80.

and sound planning, done with the blessing of career politicians, of neoliberal managerialists.

"The assassination of Paris" became the pithy thesis of Louis Chevalier's damning 1977 autopsy on Gallic urbicide, which denounced those "*polytechnicians*"—elite bureaucrats educated at France's *grandes écoles*—who'd systematically orchestrated the deadly *coup de grâce*. Like Debord, Chevalier took his native city to heart, agonized over its woes, and the former acknowledges a strange affinity.

> It could almost be believed, despite the innumerable earlier testimonies of history and the arts, that I was the only person to have loved Paris; because, first of all, I saw no one else react to this question in the repugnant seventies. But subsequently I learned that Louis Chevalier, its old historian, had published then, without too much being said about it, *The Assassination of Paris*. So we could count at least two righteous people in the city at that time.

Debord hated Le Corbusier and all he stood for. In 1925, the tyrant Swiss-cum-Parisian planner had proposed his "Voisin Plan," a vision for a modern Paris that would update Haussmann's boulevards, replacing them with a gigantic expressway grid pattern, achieving in central Paris what Robert Moses hadn't manage to achieve in lower Manhattan. Sixteen enormous skyscrapers were supposed to sprout up along the banks of the Seine, converting Paris into a thoroughly modernized radiant city, a real-life Alphaville. The plan, of course, was a non-starter; yet the mentality persisted. The highways came, like the Right-Bank expressway in 1976, baptized the "Georges-Pompidou Expressway," after the Republic's President (1969–74), gouging out the old quays of the Seine. And the towers went up, like Montparnasse, and at the westerly business node, La Défense, where Cartesian glass and steel gave public space the kiss of death.

Close by, meanwhile, the "new" city of Nanterre, "whose boredom, hideousness, rawness, whose reinforced concrete," Chevalier says in *The Assassination of Paris*, "condemned students to a kind of captivity and summed up all they detest." "The young now spit on

Paris," Chevalier laments, "Paris that had for centuries been their paradise, the city to which they flocked, convinced they would find there all they dreamed of—pleasure, love, success, glory."[17] Paris had been victim of a "*Grande Bouffe*," a greedy feast of rape and pillage, undertaken by technocrats in cahoots with a new breed of business executives, more brazenly entrepreneurial than their forebears, frequently schooled in America. Paris once stood for "people from all walks of life and all classes, people of all sorts, from high society, from the middling sort, from no society at all." Now the new consumerist Paris, the Paris of the neo-Haussmannite spectacle, "is a closed universe, disinfected, deodorized, devoid of the unexpected, without surprises, with nothing shocking, a well-protected universe."

Like Debord, Chevalier saw the destruction of Les Halles' old market halls as the violation of Paris, its real sacking, its real assassination. "With Les Halles gone," Chevalier says, "Paris has gone." February 27, 1969 proved Les Halles' last waltz, its long-dreaded last night, when Parisians must have felt the same pain that New Yorkers felt when old Penn Station was torn down three years earlier. Soon everybody was ousted, a crater hacked out, and the "hateful" Centre Pompidou crushed everything under a mountain of dust and sadness. Renzo Piano and Richard Rogers's national center of arts and culture, with its "frightful jumble of pipes and conduits and ducts," dubbed "the gas works," filled the hole but only added to the void. "It is blue," Chevalier says, "yet Paris is gray."[18] Nearby, a subterranean cave called "The Forum," "a deep, fetid underground," concentrating all that Paris had to show off as high-class merchandise, rubbed salt into the wounds. If the Sacré-Coeur trampled over the legacy of the Communards, Pompidou did likewise over *les soixante-huitards*. Debord, needless to say, abhorred the Centre Pompidou, too. In a twist of fate, the complex held a big Situationist retrospective in 1989, inviting Debord to a private viewing: he refused—unsurprisingly.

* * *

17. Louis Chevalier, *The Assassination of Paris*, University of Chicago Press, Chicago, 1994, p. 12.
18. Chevalier, *The Assassination of Paris*, p. 245.

Debord cherished Paris musty and worn, caked in dust, like a well-thumbed rare book collection that still found faithful readers. He was fascinated by the past, by the tradition of the dead generations, those weighing like a nightmare on the brain of the living. But he was also an experimental thinker and political progressive, once confessing in *In Girum Imus Nocte et Consumimur Igni*, his haunting film from 1978, a desire to "rebuild everything." Released a year after Louis Chevalier's monograph, *In Girum*'s monotone voiceover (Debord's own) utters: "It is no longer an issue between conservation and change. We were ourselves, more than anybody, the people of change, in a changing time. The owners of society were obliged, in order to sustain themselves, to change what was the inverse of ours."[19]

The Situationists were men and women of change. They were the ones who wanted to rebuild everything; but they also loved the past. They somehow wanted to go back to the future, wanted to reconstruct the best of the old world in the worst of the new, in its ruins. Debord was a man of the future yet he wanted to reconnect with the past. He wanted to bring into our modern age the epic features of former ages, and propel them into a world yet to be, a world still awaited. The incessant, eternally reoccurring, trajectory of life is precisely reflected in the motif and the film's Latin pallindromic title: "we go round and round in the night . . . ." Time flows through *In Girum* like a river always moving, in which you cannot step into twice; every ending has a new beginning, an "*à suivre*," everything begins again in a new guise. "All has gone forever," Debord says (p. 280), citing Chinese Tang poet Li Po, "everything slips away at once, events and men—like the relentless flow of the Yang-tse, which loses itself in the sea." Paris is gone forever; there is no stepping back, no second act, it's a different Seine now. The city had become an "ungovernable wasteland . . . where new sufferings disguise themselves under the name of ancient pleasures; and where people are so afraid. They go round and round in the night and are consumed by fire. They wake up alarmed, and groping, search for life. Rumor has it that those

19. Debord, "In Girum Imus Nocte Consumimur Igni," in *Oeuvres cinématographique complètes de Guy Debord*, pp. 278–9. Page numbers hereafter refer to this text. Translations are my own.

who were expropriating it have, to top it all, mislaid it. So here is a civilization that is on fire, completely capsizing and sinking."

In Girum Imus Nocte et Consumimur Igni is Debord's epic voyage brought to the screen. It is his very own *Iliad*, his *Divine Comedy*, coursing through mythical seas and plummeting into hellish realistic depths. It is a film about film—or, more accurately, a film about an anti-film. It's also a Situationist poem on the art of war, a document about the passage of time, a metaphysical exploration of Debord's mind, to say nothing of his threnody on Paris. There are aerial views of the city, panned panoramas of nocturnal Les Halles, café entrances and interiors, cellars and caves, pirates and Robin Hood, scenes of cannon fire from battleships, cavalry charges, troop formations, battlefields, Custer's last stand, the charge of the Light Brigade, all interspersed with snippets from Clausewitz and Sun Tze. The tone throughout is sad and forlorn, like a romantic refrain, like Chateaubriand's *René*, like a magnificent and terrible peace, the true taste of the passage of time. The lyrics are poetic, sublime: "Midway through the path of real life, we were surrounded by a somber melancholy, expressed in so much sad and mocking lines, in the café of lost youth [*dans le café de la jeunesse perdue*]" (p. 240).[20]

It was there where "we lived as forlorn children, our adventures incomplete." Who else, he asks, could understand the beauty of Paris apart from those who can remember its glory? Who else can know the hardships and the pleasures we knew in these places where everything has become so dire? Once, the trees weren't suffocated, the stars not extinguished by the progress of alienation. Liars have always been in power, Debord knows; but now economic development had given rulers the means to lie about everything. How could he not remember the charming hooligans and proud girls with whom he inhabited these dingy dives? "Although despising all ideological illusions, and quite indifferent to what would later prove them right,

20. In 2007, French novelist, Patrick Modiano, inspired by Debord's poetic refrain, penned *Dans le café de la jeunesse perdue*, recounting the tale of a young femme *fantomatique*, Louki, who melancholically haunts little Left Bank cafés, searching for warmth, companionship, and mislaid memories, for *souvenirs hétéroclites* of what once was and what still might be. (See Patrick Modiano, *Dans le café de la jeunesse perdue*, Gallimard, Paris, 2007.)

these reprobates had not disdained to declare openly what was to follow. To finish off art, to announce in the midst of a cathedral that God was dead, to undertake to blow up the Eiffel Tower, such were little scandals indulged in sporadically by those whose way of life was permanently such a large scandal. They pondered on why some revolutions failed; and asked if the proletariat really exists, and, if this was the case, what it could be" (p. 238).

"As for myself," Debord muses, "I have never regretted anything I have done, and I admit that I am completely unable to imagine what else I could have done, being what I am." Our formula for overthrowing the world, he says, wasn't found in books: we found it in wandering, wandering in the night. It lasted for days; nothing was like the previous day, and it never ended. It was a quest for an unholy Grail, with astonishing encounters, remarkable obstacles, grandiose betrayals, and perilous enchantments. "We hadn't aspired to subsidies for scientific research, nor to the praise of newspaper intellectuals. We carried fuel to where the fire was. It was in this matter that we definitely enlisted the Devil's party, that is to say, in this historical evil that leads the existing conditions to their destruction; through the bad side that makes history by ruining all established satisfaction" (p. 253).

They'd met "to enter into a conspiracy of limitless demands," finding themselves "enraptured with a beauty that would be swept away and which would not return." "We will soon need to leave this city that was for us so free, but which is going to fall entirely into the hands of our enemies. Already, without recourse, they're applying their blind law, remaking everything in their likeness, that is to say, on the model of a sort of cemetery." Society has always rewarded mediocrity, always rewarded those who kowtow to its unfortunate laws. "Yet I am, precisely at this time, the only person to have had some renown, clandestine and bad, and whom they haven't succeeded to get to appear on this stage of renunciation . . . I'm long practiced at living an obscure and elusive existence" (p. 259). It's a *métier* in which nobody can ever get a doctorate; so spoke our doctor of nothing, our "Prince of Division." And so the sensation of time slipped by, and the epoch that Debord loved, along with its thrills and innocence, melted away forever.

* * *

There's a telling moment in Mac Orlan's novel *La Vénus Internationale* in which Mathieu Raynold, a jaded publisher, remarks to his old friend Nicolas Gohelle: "A man lives two existences. Until the age of forty-five he absorbs the elements surrounding him. Then, all of a sudden, it's over; he doesn't absorb anything more. Thereafter he lives the duplicate of his first existence, and tries to tally the succeeding days with the rhythms and odors of his earlier active life."[21] Debord himself was trying to negotiate these two existences in *In Girum Nocte et Consumimur Igni*, a project he'd completed a little after his 45th birthday. Without maybe knowing it then, he was already tallying his retreat in the 1970s and 1980s, behind the high fortress wall of his house in Champot, with the rhythms and odors of 1950s Paris. In those Champot years, Debord writes tenderly, and complexly, perhaps even more complexly than ever before, not just about destruction but about things "he'd loved," about dear friends and comrades, about carousing till dawn. In the past, he'd been an "active adventurer," a maverick voyager, somebody who'd actively sought out novelty and change. Later, the "extreme nihilism" of his old Situationist entourage became a cherished memory, a moody melancholy; to Champot he retreated, a prince in exile, a sailor home from the sea. Thereafter, he developed into a supreme Mac Orlanian "passive adventurer," lurking with intent, within yellowing leaves, cut off from anything real or active, in a heady nether-nether continent of the unconscious, warm and safe. There, he could re-imagine and recreate his Paris as dream, as a lost twilight world of yesterday.

That's perhaps why, in the end, Debord adores Mac Orlan: Mac Orlan, after all, let Debord glimpse himself in his own living room, at Champot, at Paris's rue du Bac apartment Debord sometimes frequented in the early 1990s, where he could journey to distant shores, go to far-off urban spaces, make daring visitations, get drunk and dance, and still feel at home. And he could take you there with him. That's perhaps why Debord's politics and urbanism will never die, either, why his books and films will never date. His ideas will live

21. Pierre Mac Orlan, *La vénus internationale*, Gallimard, Paris, 1923, pp. 236–7.

on, not so much as realpolitik but as an urbanism of the imagination. Debord's life was an active voyage of discovery, engaging in covert activities here, disturbing the peace there. And yet, for all that, his enduring legacy is maybe how he tapped the mysteries of the urban unconscious, opening up its everyday heights and illuminating its nocturnal depths. Mac Orlan helped Debord retrace his steps through ruins and recapture an everyday sentimentality of an epoch of streets and hoodlums and cheap thrills. It's a realm richer and deeper than the rarified universe frequently evoked in academic studies. It's also the enduring legacy bequeathed by Guy Debord and the Situationists. For, alongside Mac Orlan, Debord understood not so much the power of the past but the tragedy of the future. "It isn't," says Mac Orlan near the end of "Montmartre," "for regretting the past that one needs to meditate on this detail, but for regretting the future."[22]

"Where are the kids of the street," Mac Orlan laments in "A Sainte-Savine," one of his popular songs for the accordion, penny poems put to music that Debord knew so well and played often on his old gramophone, "those little hoodlums of Paris / Their adolescence busted / By the prejudices of midnight? / Where are the gals of Sainte-Savine / Singing in dance halls aglow?" Good question! For the sake of an urbanism of the future, for our new urban question, you gotta hope those kids of the street, those little hoodlum gals and guys, are still in our midst, dreaming in some distant *banlieue*, mingling in its secret life, keeping those dance halls aglow.

22. Mac Orlan, "Montmartre," p. 126.

6

Urban Jacobinism

> When the government violates people's rights, insurrection is, for the people and each portion of the people, the most sacred of rights and the most indispensable of duties.
>
> —Robespierre

> The history of the revolutionary movement is, first of all, the history of the links that give it its consistency.
>
> —Agents of the Imaginary Party

One of the recurrent gripes about the movement we've come to call "Occupy"—from the mass demonstrations in Cairo's Tahrir Square to the eventual clearing out of Zuccotti Park—has been its failure to conceive a plan of action, a concerted strategy during its insurrection. There wasn't and still isn't, critics say, any strategic campaign, no coordination between particular occupations, no sense of how to amalgamate and channel all that anger and dissatisfaction into a singular, unified oppositional force—one that can stick around over the long haul. A recent salvo is Thomas Frank's in *The Baffler* magazine: "With Occupy, the horizontal culture was everything. 'The process is the message'. . . Beyond that there seems to have been virtually no strategy to speak of, no agenda to transmit to the world."[1] The other, related quip is: What comes next after the insurrection, after the good guys have assumed power, or even when they're still trying to wrestle against power? Žižek has been vocal here: "carnivals are cheap," he says. "What matters is the day after, when we will have

1. Thomas Frank, "To the Precinct Station: How Theory Met Practice . . . and Drove it Absolutely Crazy," *The Baffler*, Number 21, 2013: http://thebaffler.com/past/to_the_precinct_station.

to return to normal lives. Will there be any changes then?"[2] (Egypt, as a case in point, is still feeling the heat of a "successful" insurrection from two years ago.)

These two questions are intimately related and form part and parcel of the same *revolutionary simultaneous equation*: organizing an insurrection, consolidating it, moving through it, and, then, planning for its aftermath, putting in place something new, establishing a different set of social institutions and social relations in lieu of the old oppressive ones. (Simultaneous equations, we might remember, are equations between two unknowns, unknowns that must be solved at the same time.) This dual conundrum has preoccupied revolutionaries and revolutionary thought from time immemorial.

Walter Benjamin, we know, plotted the revolution in his own head, even while—especially while?—he lurched toward his shadow figure, Blanqui, the man of action, the arch-conspirator who spent thirty of his seventy-six years on earth in various French gaols and who was everything Benjamin wasn't: practical, fearless, ruthless. His very raison d'être was *organization*, plotting and propagandizing for the insurrection. Blanqui, Marx said, was the "head and soul" of the French workers' movement. But Blanqui satisfies only the first part of that revolutionary simultaneous equation. "The activities of a professional conspirator like Blanqui," Benjamin says, "certainly do not presuppose any belief in progress—they merely presuppose a determination to do away with present injustice. This firm resolve to snatch humanity at the last moment from the catastrophe looming at every turn is characteristic of Blanqui—more so than any other revolutionary politician of the time. He always refused to develop plans for what comes 'later'."[3]

Blanqui dreamed of a worldwide league of revolutionary communists. He also tried to put that dream into reality, countenancing conspiracy as one method for instigating insurrection. Blanqui's communism was an eclectic mix of Marxism *avant la lettre*

2. Slavoj Žižek, n+1 magazine's *Occupy!: Scenes from Occupied America*, Verso, New York, 2013.
3. Walter Benjamin, "Central Park," in Benjamin, *The Writer of Modern Life: Essays on Charles Baudelaire*, Belknap Press of Harvard University Press, Cambridge, MA, 2006, p. 166.

and heterodox anarchism, of trying to consummate the revolutionary hopes begun in 1789, yet which ended, in 1794, in Thermidorian backlash. In the mid-nineteenth century Blanqui tried to reset those earlier hopes of the Revolution, reacting against Thermidor reaction. Still, as Samuel Bernstein cautions in *Auguste Blanqui and the Art of Insurrection*, Blanqui "couldn't adjust himself to an organization of huge dimensions. It rendered absurd his strategy of insurrection; and it placed in the foreground the working class which he had never regarded as a key propeller of history."[4] Instead, Blanqui's political organization was limited in size, tightly pulled together, hierarchical in structure, made "like a seamless garment, programmatically homogeneous, disciplined, obedient, and ready to move."[5] Blanqui's insurrection was vertically organized yet spread itself out horizontally, immanently entering daily life, not so much a factory struggle as an urban war, a civil war rooted above all else—or below all else—in the street.[6]

* * *

The key organizing medium for Blanquists was the "Society of the Seasons," formed in the 1830s when Marx was still a fresh-faced lad. The society met clandestinely; leaders went unseen; meetings recruited foot soldiers who'd form an army of revolt, ready for action, likely violent action. The Society's network barely stretched beyond Paris; but its covert nature of cells unnerved the powers that be and meant the Society punched above its weight, or at least threatened to.

---

4. Samuel Bernstein, *Auguste Blanqui and the Art of Insurrection*, Lawrence and Wishart, London, 1971, p. 307.
5. Bernstein, *Auguste Blanqui and the Art of Insurrection*, p. 307.
6. A great collection of Blanqui's writings and missives has been put together by Dominique Nuz in *Maintenant, il faut des armes* [*Now, we need weapons*] (Éditions la fabrique, Paris, 2006), from which I have drawn in my thoughts on Blanqui—his theory and practice. The assorted texts have a fascinating preface by "agents of the Imaginary Party," those anonymous authors of *The Coming Insurrection*. Blanqui also has a brilliant biographer, Gustave Geffroy, whose *L'enfermé avec le masque de Blanqui* (Eugène Fasquelle, Paris, 1919) remains classic reading for all "republican communists."

In Blanqui's time, these Society of the Seasons were the revolutionary Jacobin clubs 40 years down the line. (Blanqui may have disagreed: In his early career he admired the "Incorruptible" Jacobin, Robespierre, but later claimed he was really a Hébertist, a descendent of the radical eighteenth-century journalist Jacques-René Hébert.)

Blanqui knew, just as Robespierre knew, just as any revolutionary today must soberly know, that if an insurrection were to succeed, and consolidate itself afterward, it would have to muster support from the *faubourgs*, from the *banlieues*, from the peripheral hinterlands. We might see any society of revolutionaries nowadays similarly needing to establish cells in the *banlieues*, cells within urban cells, revolutionary activity flowing through the capillaries and arteries of our global urban fabric, through its physical and fiber-optic infrastructure, through its hardware and thoughtware. These secret cells must plot to stymie the dominant flow of things and will likely be spearheaded by professional organizers and tacticians, by black bloc'er anarchists, by socialists and autonomous communists of different stripes and persuasions, by anonymous rookies, by those who've never been politically active before, by men and women, blacks and whites, young *casseurs* and *voyous* (and *voyelles*), by everybody who, with Occupy, with the Arab Spring, with the revolt in the *banlieues*, with the ongoing urban civil war everywhere, with growing unemployment, have found some medium to channel and refract their energies and dissatisfactions.

Perhaps there's a neo-Jacobinism blowing in wind, not quite bawling out but certainly getting whispered, a revival of Jacobin values with its great desire to abolish slavery in our urban neo-colonies, to denounce aristocratic plenty and root for *sans-culotte* empowerment. In 2010, *Jacobin: A Magazine of Culture and Polemic* was launched in the U.S. by a young socialist-journalist Bhaskar Sunkara; the mag attempts to tap a younger radical readership, urging people "to modify your dissent," to turn the screw against neoliberalism, to tame the shrew. Within its pages Žižek has already invoked "The Jacobin Spirit," defending Robespierre and his "virtue of violence." (See, for more provocations, Žižek's presentation of *Robespierre: Virtue and Terror* [Verso, London, 2007], and Sophie Wahnich's *In Defense of Terror* [Verso, London, 2012].) Meanwhile, French radical publisher La fabrique not so long ago published the selected writings of Robespierre—*Robespierre: pour le bonheur et pour la libérté* [for happiness and for liberty] [Éditions la fabrique, 2013]: "*citoyens, voulez-vous une révolution sans révolution?*"; and a biography by Georges Labica, first published in 1990, and reissued through the same house in 2013: *Robespierre: une politique de la philosophie*. "*La Révolution n'est pas terminée*," warns editor Eric Hazan, mischievously, in his blurb.

The Jacobin club was founded on the eve of Revolution, in a Dominican convent on the Seine's Right Bank, along rue Saint-Honoré. Meetings there were secret debating societies made up of left-leaning deputies, republican enemies of the monarchy who'd push for the constitution of 1791. The club bore the noble label "Society of Friends of Liberty and Equality." Later it opened its membership to small storeowners and artisans. Over 5,000 clubs operated throughout France; pamphlets and newspapers got published; rallies and processions organized. After the fall of the monarchy, Robespierre led the Jacobins in the National Convention. The revolutionary fervor of the Jacobins came through its popularism, through the support of the *sans-culottes*, "those beings," a 1793 archive says, "who go everywhere on foot, who at no point have millions in the bank, nor a chateau, nor valets at their beck and call; who lodge simply and at night present themselves to their section . . . applying all their force to pulverize those who come from that abominable faction of stately men." And those stately men, the aristocrats? "They're the rich," another 1793 document says, "all those fat merchants, all the monopolizers, the mountebanks, the bankers, all the swindlers and all those who have something." Sound familiar?

And a "Society of Friends of Liberty and Equality," a neo-Jacobin radicalism today that's as organized and offensive as its namesake from the 1790s? Why not? This time, though, any society would really need to be "popular," would need to open its doors to all types of *sans-culottes*, and of all genders. Meeting halls, debating chambers and political networks might be less grandiose: in cafés and on street corners, in estates and at youth centers, in universities classrooms and at mall bowling alleys, anywhere where young people hang out; dialogue might be online as well as face-to-face; a society of "friends" puts another egalitarian spin on Facebook camaraderie. A contra-Tea Party that drinks fair-trade coffee.

But let's be clear: secrecy would be paramount in these meetings, certainly initially, during the plotting, given how the forces of law and order mercilessly cracks down on all subversive politicking. We've heard about how the FBI infiltrated Occupy Wall Street (OWS), tracked known activists and student radicals, even on college campuses. The "Partnership for Civil Justice Fund" (PCJF), a U.S. watchdog civil rights group, recently blew the whistle when they obtained FBI documents: "from its inception," PCJF say, "the FBI treated the Occupy movement as a potential criminal and terrorist threat." FBI offices and agents, "were in high gear conducting surveillance against the movement even as early as August 2011, a month prior to the establishment of the OWS encampment in Zuccotti Park and other Occupy actions around the country." And in France, especially in the *banlieues*, the "Brigade anticriminalité" (BAC), overtly and covertly, has intensified "special police units" patrolling "*les zones sensibles*." As Mathieu Rigouste writes in *La domination policière* (La fabrique, 2012), "the generalization of the BAC in urban territories is one of the decisive stamps of the counter-insurrectional restructuring of the police."

If anything, "austerity" these days has become a veritable 9/11 in Europe: a watchword, in other words, for neoliberal governments to quieten any dissenting voice. In Greece, where austerity has been most brutally implemented, "centers of lawlessness" have been nipped in the bud. In January 2013, two longstanding "occupied" social centers in Athens, Villa Amalias and Skaramanga, with over 100 makeshift residents, were summarily evicted; and former denizens promptly arrested in a relentless police war of attrition, "Operation Zeus," against all those outside the dominant orthodoxy, including undocumented migrants. In *Al Jazeera* newspaper, Antonis Vradis reports from the frontline: "The eviction of Villa Amalias and the forthcoming police operation," Vradis says, "reveals what is an inescapable contradiction in the reformulation of power in the Greek territory: In its short-term quest for stability, it is accelerating long-term social and political change."[7]

7. www.aljazeera.com/indepth/opinion/2013/01/2013115105715250554.html.

* * *

Against such short-term desperation for stability comes, then, an urgent and accelerated need for social and political change. Any Jacobin revival has to take us into and through the insurrection; and it has to leave us with something to build upon on the other side, in its aftermath. Which leads us to the second part of our revolutionary simultaneous equation. One of the amazing things Eric Hazan points out in *Une histoire de la révolution française*, his fresh, partisan take on an old story—the French Revolution—is how quickly it all happened, how fast an immense and deeply entrenched power structure and administration evaporated, caved in, without neither warning nor transition. Hazan evokes the spirit of the Jacobin club, as much about what it might still be as what it once was: "the Society and its affiliates functioned as a system of diffusion of radical ideas. Nothing is more absurd than the notion of 'Jacobinism' as an authoritarian Parisian dictatorship. That's a fabrication inherited from the [counter-revolutionary] Thermidor, which endures along with a hatred of the Revolution."[8]

Hazan devotes memorable, generous lines—again with the same spirit of going back to the future—to the National Convention, the first revolutionary assembly elected through universal (male) suffrage. "Was the Convention representative of the people?" Hazan asks. If considered as an electoral system, he says, which is to say, as a system of participatory democracy, then clearly not. Yet the virtues of the Convention, as well as its suggestive, enduring visionary politics, came and might still come through an altogether different means. To be sure, the Convention is still unprecedented in how it allowed ordinary people to intervene in its sittings. That ordinary citizens and not a few *sans-culottes* could pass through the hollowed gates of Parliamentary politics was remarkable then and almost unthinkable now.

Although the Convention's "Salle du Manège" was limited in size, it did manage to receive three thousands citizens at any one time;

8. Eric Hazan, *Une histoire de la révolution française*, Éditions la fabrique, Paris, 2012, pp. 88–9.

and at tribunals, says Hazan, ordinary folk "didn't hesitate to noisily speak out their opinion"; deputies were forced to respond on the spot and were directly answerable to peoples' plain outspokenness, to interrogation from their constituents. Alongside this popular participation, sittings of the Convention kicked off by listening to peoples' letters, often voicing long commentaries on deputies' propositions, offering suggestions, sympathetic encouragement, angry critique. "In this regard," concludes Hazan, "the Convention is the first and only national assembly where the people had been able to have their voice directly heard."[9]

So a message rings out, loud and jarringly: what an insurrection needs to do is force those Parliamentary doors open, smash them down if necessary, so that "the people" gain access. Not so much a participatory government as the chance for a real representative assembly, one in which elected politicians, for the first time in centuries, would actually be responsive to their electorate, engaging with them within an open democratic structure; they'd be answerable, in other words, to the populace not to the usual powerful suspects.

But how to keep counter-revolutionary economic and political interests at bay, how to justifiably shut them out of any new Convention, how to *ruthlessly* shut them out if necessary? The theme of violence inevitably enters the scene, the idea that there's a legitimate violence responsive to the everyday violence initiated by the forces of law and order, from its judiciary to its paramilitary, from its surveillance and containment to the outright wars it wages against people its power base doesn't like. War, from the dominant standpoint, is a just-in-case response, a strike-first-ask-questions-later initiative, a branch of "democracy" that needs to construct its own inconceivable foe: *terrorists*. Guy Debord confirmed as much back in 1988: "Its wish is to be judged by its enemies rather than by its results." "People must certainly never know everything about terrorism," says Debord, "but they must always know enough to convince them that, compared with terrorism, everything else must be acceptable."[10]

---

9. Hazan, *Une histoire de la révolution française*, p.186.
10. Guy Debord, *Comments on the Society of the Spectacle*, Verso, London, 1991, p. 24.

More than 200 years after Robespierre's execution, an ideological logic lives on in governments around the world, one that defiles the Jacobin legacy, panders to a revisionist, right-wing Thermidorian telling of the truth: Robespierre was a bloody tyrant, a fanatical monster, a terrorist butcher. And yet, as Eric Hazan maintains, "Robespierre took positions of great coherence and astonishing courage—positions where he was always a minority and sometimes *absolutely alone*: against *suffrage censitaire* [census suffrage], for civic rights of actors and Jews, against martial law, against slavery in the colonies, against the death penalty, for the right to petition, for the freedom of the press . . . In what country, in what assembly, have we ever heard so much *contre-courant* argument declared with such force of conviction?"[11] Robespierre was defiled, still is defiled, because what he said threatened ruling class privilege, upset their status quo; to defile him thus serves to tarnish every future hope of revolution, of future social change. "I was born to fight crime," he says in a final speech from 1794. "The time has not arrived for men of substance to be able to serve their homeland with impunity; defenders of liberty will be outlaws, for as long as the horde of scoundrels predominates."[12]

The new urban question is about creating a Jacobin movement that can contest the "horde of scoundrels" who still predominate, that can stand up to their arsenal and ideologues; a movement that can loosen the neo-Haussmannite grip on our society and declares war against its protagonists and puppets. Manuel Castells saw the old urban question as a question answered by "urban social movements" struggling for their right to the city; yet the new urban question needs to be countered by something much more expansive, something much more far-reaching: by an urban *political* movement that struggles for generalized democracy, that organizes a concerted insurrection; and, moreover, knows exactly what it's fighting *for* as well as against. To do so we need visionaries as well as agitators, conspirators like Blanqui but also leaders like Robespierre, people with big plans and grand convictions—outlaw mathematicians who know, perhaps more than anything else, all about solving revolutionary simultaneous equations.

---

11. Hazan, *Une Histoire de la révolution française*, p. 356.
12. Robespierre, "Extracts from Speech of 8th Thermidor, Year II" cited in Slavoj Žižek, *Robespierre: Virtue and Terror*, Verso, London 2007, p. 141.

7

Old Discourse on New Inequality

What would Jean-Jacques Rousseau, who penned his classic *Discourse on Inequality* in 1755, have made of things today? Had he still been around, had he travelled around the globe a bit, typically critical and inquiring, he'd have doubtless despaired of how little "civilized" society had ameliorated the "artificial" inequalities that derive from the conventions that govern us. Here's Rousseau, proud citizen of Geneva, speaking 34 years before the French Revolution, a revolution he supposedly helped author, yet never lived to see himself: "one sees a handful of powerful and rich men on the pinnacle of grandeur and fortune, while the crowd grovels in obscurity and wretchedness." "A handful of people gorge themselves with superfluities while a multitude goes in want of necessities."[1] "Luxury, impossible to prevent among men who are greedy for their own comforts and for consideration from others, soon completes the damage that societies begin, and on the pretext of keeping alive the poor, a pretext of which there is no need, luxury impoverishes everyone else, and sooner or later depopulates the state" (p. 151). If we can believe Rousseau, what's happened between "nascent society," and the subsequent maturity of advanced urban society, has been a "fraudulent social contract," imposed upon the poor by the rich. And somehow, in assorted shapes and forms, we've been living out that fraud ever since.

Had Rousseau still been around, maybe he'd have also played a cameo role in a recent hit documentary, *Inequality for All*, directed by Jacob Kornbluth with economist Robert Reich as the unlikely

1. Jean-Jacques Rousseau, *A Discourse on Inequality*, Penguin, London, 1984, p. 137.

lead. (Rousseau's appearance would have only been cameo, of course, because later in life he avoided the limelight he'd courted as a young man; and he was a reluctant public orator, despite being a dab hand at voicing inconvenient public truths.) *Inequality for All* follows Reich teaching his packed undergraduate class on "Wealth and Poverty" at the University of California, Berkeley. In 1978, Reich says, your typical U.S. male worker doing just fine was pulling in around $48,000 a year; your boss back then was probably making around $390,000. Thirty-odd years on, in 2010, the former struggles to earn $33,000 a year, while the latter's average annual share has bloated to well over a million bucks.[2]

Union busting, wage depreciation and market deregulation have led to huge hikes in national wealth but little has trickled down. Rather, it's been creamed off by skyrocketing executive salaries, by super-inflated bonuses and massive payoffs for serially failing company bosses and no-mark bankers. The number of billionaires, unsurprisingly, has risen exponentially; and six-figure earner tax rates frequently dip under 10 percent, against the 30 percent for your average stiff. Costs of living, meanwhile, continue to soar—costs of everyday commodities, costs of housing, costs of healthcare (in both the U.K. and U.S.), and costs of education. "Where America leads," Reich says, "the rest of the world follows. This same thing is affecting people all over the world. If nothing is done to reverse this trend, Britain will find itself in exactly the same place as America in just a few years' time." Indeed, as at December 2010, 10 percent of the fattest cats in the U.K. own 40 percent of the national wealth; and Royal Bank of Scotland investment bankers, after finagling Libor interest-rates, now apparently contemplate awarding themselves bonuses in excess of £250 million. And in April 2013, payouts for corporate honchos amounted to £1.7 billion *higher* than the same month a year prior (2012), "with banks and finance accounting for £700 million of the increase." Adding injury to popular insult, financiers in the U.K. delayed cashing in these huge bonuses until Chancellor's tax cuts for

2. See Carole Cadwalladr, "Inequality for All: Another Inconvenient Truth?," *Observer*, 2 February 2013.

top earners became operative![3] (Wait a minute. Are we talking about those failure bankers who embezzle our money and fuck up on the job? I guess we are!)

And just when it's needed most, a strong state turns cowardly, has desisted from holding out a safety net. In many ways, that net has so many large holes in now that any falling object slips through. Now, states have systematically backed off from funding those public goods—"collective consumption" goods—items consumed collectively, like transport and utilities, like hospitals and schools and public spaces. The state has capitulated, restructured itself in times of "austerity," the latest buzzword for neoliberal governance not only to step back from addressing concerns of inequality, but in a lot of ways to directly perpetuate inequality; because, now, states have sold off these collectively owned goods to private capital at knockdown prices; and sometimes at no price at all.

Never before has growth—particularly urban growth—depended so centrally on the creation of new mechanisms to wheel and deal finance capital and credit money, on new deregulated devices, underwritten by the state, for looting and finagling, for absorbing surplus capital into real estate speculation. These days capital accumulation predicates itself not so much on production as such but on *dispossession*, on expropriation—an alternative growth strategy a lot more creatively destructive than in Marx's day; now it offers fresh terrains for speculation and market expansion: asset-stripping through mergers and acquisitions, pension funds raiding, biopiracy and privatization of hitherto common assets (like water and power utilities); all told, a general pillaging of publicly-owned property.

Our old friend Baron Haussmann once tore into central Paris, into its old neighborhoods and poorer populations, dispatching the latter to the periphery as he speculated on the center; the built urban form became simultaneously a property machine and a means to divide and rule; today, neo-Haussmannization, as I've been calling it, is a process that likewise integrates financial, corporate and state interests, yet tears into the globe and seizes land through forcible

3. "Top Earners Cash in on Tax Cut by Delaying Bonuses Worth £1.7bn," *Guardian*, August 21, 2013.

slum clearance and a handy vehicle for dispossession known as "eminent domain." Once, seemingly long ago, this latter act of public sequestration was done, albeit disruptively, in the name of some greater common good—you know, like commandeering land that'd eventually be used for public infrastructure. Now, it expresses the public sector expropriating land and then giving it away for upscale private re-appropriation, letting private economic interests cash in on legalized looting. Many urban areas the world over have seen the greatest land grab in history, when big corporate money obtain at practically no cost great swaths of land for redevelopment.

Which promptly begs the question: Whose austerity? Even a cursory glance at the bourgeois press (circa February 2013) reveals bundles. European Union leaders, we hear, began "marathon talks" in Brussels about new budget plans that "reflect the climate of austerity across a continent still struggling to emerge from a crippling debt crisis." The task, in other words, is to hammer down public spending, to hammer down public services, to hammer down public sector jobs and pay—seemingly while private sector spending has no limits, no ceiling, not even a glass one. Indeed, that same week as EU bigwigs debated austerity, Michael Bloomberg (no stranger to imposing austerity on his Big Apple fiefdom—cf. his recent clampdown of school bus driver pay raises) negotiated extending his billion-dollar empire "over the pond," in London, in a major new expansion in what will be one of the U.K.'s most prestigious locations, Bloomberg Place in Kensington. And in Bloomberg's London home at Cadogan Square, Mayor Mike is spending over $20 million alone on installing air-conditioning. This at the same time as Ibrahim Ibrahimov, another of those "handful" of the world's wealthiest billionaires, spearheads his $100 billion dream project of developing 55 islands and the world's tallest tower in the Caspian Sea. (The tower itself will cost $3 billion.) And, to cap it all, February 2013 was a good month for the luxury art market: Sotheby's sold 52 works for £121 million, and Christie's auctioned a stand-alone Modigliani for £27 million.

* * *

Rousseau would have found these data, headlines, and news tidbits interesting curiosities rather than anything particularly shocking; they were nothing his intuitive reason wouldn't have already known, wouldn't have already felt, felt in the air.[4] He'd have probably seen the like around any urban neighborhood, out on a daily peregrination, when he'd ruminate on foot and "apply his barometer to the soul of men," himself included. ("I have never been able to write or think with any ease," he says in *Confessions*, "except in the open air . . . as soon as I stop, I can no longer think, for my mind moves only when my feet do."[5]) Rousseau wasn't voicing grim empirical truths about inequality that everyday people already knew anyway, from their working (and non-working) lives; his spirit was much more inventive and imaginative than that, much more original and radical, instinctively and spontaneously stirring up trouble. He was neither economist nor empiricist: he didn't need "evidence" to back up his own structure of feeling reality, his own way of grasping and groping reality; his knowledge came from a certain perception of things, not from a certain measurement of things; it was no less meaningful for all that. We might even see Rousseau alongside Lefebvre and Benjamin: as one of our metaphilosophers of the city—despite him sometimes holding powerful anti-urban sentiments. Though as Sébastien Mercier points out in *Le tableau de Paris* [1788], while "Rousseau's imagination dwelt only in meadows, waters and woods, with their animated solitude . . . as he approached the age of sixty, he returned [in 1770] to live in Paris, in rue Plâtrière, in other words, the most noisy, uncomfortable, crowded and diseased of bad places."[6]

When Rousseau writes in his "second discourse" about inequality he does so as a moralist and philosopher. (Rousseau's "first discourse" won Dijon Academy's prize in 1751 for best essay "on the science and arts," on whether progress in each had improved human morals;

---

4. Still one of the best evocations of Rousseau's authentic spirit of feeling reason is the late Marshall Berman's first book, *The Politics of Authenticity* (Atheneum Books, New York, 1970). See, especially, the chapter "A New Politics: The Authentic Citizen," pp. 200–8.
5. Jean-Jacques Rousseau, *The Confessions*, Oxford University Press, Oxford, 2000, p. 400.
6. Cited in Eric Hazan, *The Invention of Paris*, p. 76.

Rousseau's response was a categoric NO!) Rousseau wasn't so much interested in analyzing the facts as speculating on causes, causes that are, he says, rooted in human behavior, in humanly created institutions, which seem to take on a life of their own, alienating people, dispossessing masses of men and women of their inner selves and inner worth. Thus, for Rousseau, inequality spells a loss of human potentiality and dignity.

Corruption isn't inevitable in itself; people are corruptible, he says, only in a certain context, in a context like ours that seems to reward those who do the least for society and the most for themselves. In many ways Rousseau's discourse anticipates Marx's "Economic and Philosophical Manuscripts," written almost a century later, laying bare the corrupting "power of money": "I am bad, dishonest, unscrupulous, stupid," says Marx, "but money is honored, and therefore so is its possessor. Money is the supreme good, therefore its possessor is good. Money, besides, saves me the trouble of being dishonest: I am therefore presumed honest. I am stupid, but money is the real mind of all things and how then should its possessor be stupid?"[7]

Both Rousseau and Marx see private property as fueling human vanity, as provoking, in Rousseau's words, "the usurpations of the rich and the brigandage of the poor"; "war begins," says Rousseau in *Discourse on Inequality* (p. 41), "when the idea of property is born and one man claims as his own what another man's hunger prompts him to seize." Unlike Marx, though, Rousseau isn't against private property per se: he's against a culture that rewards accumulating property and wealth, and the human instinct that seems to prop up that selfish passion: *amour-propre*, Rousseau famously calls it, or "pride," self-centered greed, a haughty desire to be superior to everybody else. To have self-esteem or even self-love—*amour de soi-même*—is one thing; but *amour-propre* (pride) is another thing again. "Self-love is a natural sentiment," Rousseau says in one of his numerous, lengthy footnotes to *Discourse on Inequality* (pp. 167–8), "which prompts every animal to watch over its own conservation";

7. Karl Marx, "The Economic and Philosophical Manuscripts," in *Early Writings*, Penguin, Harmondsworth, 1978, p. 377.

"pride," on the other hand, "is only a relative, artificial sentiment born in society, a sentiment which prompts each individual to attach more importance to himself than to anyone else, which inspires all the injuries men do to themselves and others."

But Rousseau's morality play about property and pride has decisive *political* implications; always his views have decisive political implications. "I had seen that everything is rooted in politics," he says in *Confessions*, "and that, whatever the circumstances, a people will never be other than the nature of its government makes it. In other words, that great question, as to which is the best possible form of government, seemed to me to come down in the end to this one: what is the nature of the government most likely to produce the most virtuous, the most enlightened, the wisest, and in short, taking this word in its widest sense, the best people?"[8]

* * *

Rousseau was a strange, restless autodidact who never seemed to fit in anywhere for very long. He was a republican contemptuous of the *ancien régime* with its prissy courtiers, and of an ascendant bourgeoisie with its wealth of nations, a standpoint that brought him much closer to Diderot than to Voltaire. Rousseau abhorred old and new money alike—well, almost alike, because he cozied up to the former for pastoral refuge. Rousseau's vision of a new social contract, in which liberty and law coexist in equal measure, coexist to support and reinforce one another, is a system of governance that tears off its aristocratic fetters at the same time as it moves beyond the conceit (and fraud) of bourgeois liberal democracy—as he and we still know it. It's a vision that continues to challenge us to see things in a different way.

The world Robert Reich describes in *Inequality for All* as a pre-1978 regime now seems like our very own *ancien régime* when we had the middle-classes bookended by working classes on the poorer side—with a lumpenproletariat at the very fringes of that side—and a bourgeoisie on the other much richer side. But today this

8. Rousseau, *Confessions*, p. 395.

"much richer" side has taken a peculiar turn. In our *nouveau régime*, members of the upper bourgeoisie have risen to such prominence, have accumulated such wealth and power, that now they assume the mantle of an astonishingly rich, new-monied group of people who behave like a veritable class of old feudal lords, presiding not only over particular companies, but over whole national and supra-international governments as well. (Half of U.S. assets, remember, are owned by just 400 people.) Correspondingly, a big chunk of the middle ground has caved in, imploded, and a "moral depreciation" (as Marx labeled economically redundant fixed capital) has been inflicted on real living human beings; meaning these middling types have slipped into the ranks of the *sans-culottes*, finding it evermore difficult to make ends meet, just as the top 1 percent has decoupled itself from the rest of us. And while the absolute exploitation of labor remains an evident string in the bow of this rich aristocracy, more often than not they're now the bearers of flows of merchant and rentier capital, gouging profits from unequal exchanges and interest-bearing assets, as well as from rents accruing from monopoly land control.

In one of the great works on the French Revolution, *Les sans-culottes* [1968], Albert Soboul points to the influence Rousseau exerted on the revolutionary throng, even if few from this throng had actually read his great texts. Somehow his republican ideals were immanent in the epoch, voiced and debated in the Jacobin societies, but also lived out and practiced by the popular masses. Robespierre, a close reader, worshipped Rousseau; Rousseau, the former said, was his *maître* and teacher; and Robespierre endorsed the Swiss citizen's sovereignty of the "general will," together with the notion that any Republic can survive only with a measure of social equality. Soboul cites one citizen from 1793 saying: "According to the Geneva philosopher [Rousseau], the social state was no use to man 'unless everyone had something and no one had too much.' Whereas it is true that an equitable distribution of money can be looked upon as being an illusion by anyone of intelligence, it is nevertheless also true that the monstrous disproportion that exists between the proud millionaire [and proud billionaire] and the humble wage earner cannot be permitted much longer in the new order of things."[9]

And in that "new order of things" the legitimacy of popular insurrection is inalienable; Rousseau declares the like: "The insurrection which ends with the strangling or dethronement of a sultan," he says, toward the *dénounement* to *A Discourse on Inequality*, "is just as lawful an act as those by which he disposed the day before of the lives and property of his subjects. Force alone maintained him; force alone overthrows him."[10] And yet, as Soboul confirms (p. 256), the *sans-culottes* weren't a class as such: instead they comprised, perhaps still comprise, artisans and small shopkeepers, modest merchants and "journeymen . . . [and women] day laborers—along with a bourgeois minority," those, we might say, who've slipped into the popular ranks and are beginning to know it.

The *sans-culottes* represented an irresistible force undergirding a coalition collectively consciousness of a common enemy; it was a strategic alliance that recognized and needs still to recognize a common revolutionary project—similar to yet different from 1789. For now the revolutionary insurrection must rid itself of a new aristocracy without having a liberal bourgeoisie step in in its stead. The revolutionary movement against economic absolutism needs, then, the *sans-culottes* leading the way, retaining its hatred of the aristocracy while being forever leery of well-meaning short-term reformism. A passionate desire for equality might cue this militancy and get debated in any emergent Jacobin society. Meanwhile, a new social contract needs drafting, initially in pencil, before getting definitively rubber-stamped in ink in the streets, in the new and necessary citizens' agoras we've yet to invent.

9. Albert Soboul, *The Sans-Culottes*, Princeton University Press, Princeton NJ, 1980, p. 57.
10. Rousseau, *Discourse on Inequality*, p. 135.

8

Every Revolution has Its Agora

In *The Social Contract* (1762), near the end of the "Social Compact" [*pacte social*] section, there's a footnote added by the author. In it, Rousseau qualifies what he means by the idea (and ideal) of *citizen*, of how it embodies a particular territorial disposition, and how, "in modern times," "the real meaning of the word has been almost wholly lost."[1] The footnote has one of the most famously quotable lines from *The Social Contract*: "houses make a town, but citizens make a city." (The most famously quotable, of course, is the opening refrain: "humans are born free; and everywhere they're in chains.") The notion that "houses make a town, but citizens make a city" is the standard English riff on Rousseau's original French, passed down the historical line, unchanged and unchallenged. The phrase gets preceded by this musing: "most people mistake a town for a city, and a townsman for a citizen" (p. 192).

Now, maybe it's just me, but in our own modern times there's something woefully inadequate about this translation; and Rousseau's concern about losing the real meaning of citizen seems more prescient than even he might have ever imagined. Worse, the standard translation hints of a certain bourgeois re-appropriation and makes Rousseau's radical text sound a lot less radical than it might still be. So let's consider his original text more closely: "*la plupart prennent une ville pour une cité, et un bourgeois pour un citoyen. Ils ne savent pas que les maisons font la ville, mais que les citoyens font la cité.*"[2] These two sentences, it's true, pose difficulty for any Anglo translator. Not least because the word "town" doesn't really exist

---

1. Jean-Jacques Rousseau, *The Social Contract*, Dent, London, 1973, p. 192.
2. Jean-Jacques Rousseau, *Du contrat social*, Éditions Sociales, Paris, 1968, p. 68.

in French: *petite ville* is often its everyday usage, a small city, but Rousseau isn't using the word *petite ville*; he says, quite clearly, *ville*. On the other hand, *cité* has no direct equivalent in English. And yet, if we move beyond semantics and get into the spirit of Rousseau's intended meaning, the standard translation might satisfy political scientists and philosophers, but it can no longer be acceptable for radical political urbanists.

For a start, "town" is a much too archaic term, and a much too limited (and redundant) political jurisdiction to have meaning for a contemporary reader; and so, too, is "city" a problematic basis for a "modern" concept of citizenship. *Cité*, though, does continue to speak in loud political decibels, yet only if its domain is reconsidered imaginatively, perhaps even normatively. In that sense, here's how a contemporary urbanist, a contemporary philosopher and metaphilosopher of the urban, might recalibrate Rousseau: "the majority [of people] take a city for the *cité* and a bourgeois for a citizen." (Rousseau, we might note, uses the politically charged "bourgeois" not benign "townsman"; he knew that it took—and still takes—more than a bunch of rich and influential folks to comprise a real citizenry.) He continues: people "don't know that houses make a city, but citizens make a *cité*." I've left this notion of *cité* untranslated for the moment because it's the part that needs a refreshed vocabulary, a contemporary reloading. And this is what I'd like to propose and develop as a working hypothesis: "the majority [of people] take a city for the *cité*, and a bourgeois for a citizen. They don't know that houses make a city but citizens make the urban [*la cité*]."

The urban, in other words, might be better suited for Rousseau's notion of *cité*: it satisfies more accurately, and maybe more radically, a politically charged concept of citizenship that goes beyond nationality and flag waving. (*Cité*, we might equally note, raises the "popular" specter in bourgeois circles, pejoratively evoking *quartiers des sans-culottes*, the no-go *zones sensibles* and global *banlieues*, neighborhoods dreaded by the ruling classes.) For the physical and social manifestation of our landscape, for its bricks and mortar, we have what most people would deem "city." But as a political ideal, as a new social contract around which citizenship might cohere, we have something we might call "the urban"; a more expansive realm for which no passports are required and around which people the world over might bond. Citizenship might here be conceived as something urban, as something territorial, yet one in which territoriality is both narrower and broader than both "city" and "nationality"; a territory and citizenship without borders.

So maybe the idea of *cité*—a territory both real and ideal—satisfies the jurisdictional ideal of Rousseau's *Social Contract*: the living space of modern democracy in the making. That's why there are no passports for Rousseauian citizens of the urban universe, no passports for those who know they *live* somewhere yet *feel* they belong everywhere. Or who want to feel it. This conjoining of knowing and feeling is what engenders a sense of empathy whose nom de plume might really be citizenship itself. Here we might take the notion of "dwelling" in its broadest sense: as the totality of political and economic space in which one now belongs. The urban helps affinity grow, helps it become aware of itself, aware that other affinities exist in the world, that affinities can encounter one another, become aware of one another as *sans-culottes*, as the 99%, in a social network connected by a certain tissuing, by a spider's webbing, by a planetary webbing: an affinity of urban citizenship; houses make a city, but citizens make *la cité*.

The people's "general will" today can only ever express itself within this urban [*cité*] context. The general will [*la volonté générale*] is the sum of affinities taking shape, an expression of dissatisfaction en masse, perhaps at first knowing better what this will doesn't like, what it's against, than what it's actually for. At any rate, Rousseau's logic is rather beautiful: the general will of the people, he explains, is both infallible and fallible: "The general will is always upright and always tends to the public advantage; but it doesn't follow that the deliberations of the people always have the same rectitude. Our will is always for our own good, but we don't always see what it is; the people is never corrupted, but it is often deceived, and on such occasions only does it seem to will what is bad."[3] Yet how might this general will work itself out? And how might the common urban affinities that cement people together actually develop today? Where might

3. Rousseau, *Social Contract*, p. 203.

these affinities, and this general will, emerge? How can particular wills be made aware of themselves as something more general, as a larger collective constituency that's something greater than the sum of individual parts? What are the institutions through which affinity might develop? A direct response to these questions might be: in the *citizens' agora*, in the space of the urban, in the popular realm where a public might come together and express itself as a unanimous general will.

* * *

The citizens' agora is something more than the public spaces of the city, more, even, than the public institutions we once knew as public—state institutions forever under fire. One reason for this is that it isn't clear anymore just what the public domain constitutes, what it is, let alone what it might be. In our day, the public realm hasn't so much fallen from grace as gone into whole-scale tailspin. Eighty-odd years after *The Social Contract*, and almost 60 after the 9th Thermidor counter-revolution, Marx, in *The Communist Manifesto*, demonstrated what liberal bourgeois democracy had bequeathed us: "no other nexus between man and man than naked self-interest, than callous cash payment . . . drowning the most heavenly ecstasies of . . . chivalrous enthusiasm, of philistine sentimentalism, in the icy water of egotistical calculation." Bourgeois society, Marx says, "has resolved personal [and public] worth into exchange value," and rips away halos of every sort, converting all erstwhile hallowed and holy realms, including the public realm itself, into another money realm, into another means to accumulate capital. Marx, in a nutshell, leaves us with the rather bleak task of picking up the pieces of what the public realm might still mean.[4]

There's a consequent need to redefine not a public realm that's collectively owned and managed by the state, but a public realm of

4. Marx and Engels, *The Communist Manifesto*, Penguin Deluxe Edition, New York, 2011, p. 67. This very lovely rendering of the *Manifesto*, incidentally, is introduced by Marshall Berman and is adorned with French cartoonist Patrice Killoffer's brilliant artwork.

the *cité* that is somehow *expressive* of the people, expressive of the general will—a will, maybe, that incorporates an affinity of *common notions*, notions that Spinoza always insisted were not universal notions, not universal rights. Spinoza was against such an abstract conception of universality, which he thought was an *inadequate idea*. Common notions are general rather than abstract, general in their practical and contextual applicability. From this standpoint, when something is public, its channels for common expression remain open, negotiable and debatable, political in the sense that "public" witnesses people encountering other people, dialoguing with other people, arguing with other people, formulating an infallible general will.

Twenty-first-century urban spaces of the *cité* will then be public spaces not for reasons of pure concrete physicality or centrality, nor even because of land tenure, but because they are meeting places between virtual and physical worlds, between online and offline conversations, between online and offline encounters. Space won't so much be divided between public and private as between *passive* or *active*; between a space that encourages active encounters of people and a space that resigns itself to passive encounters, not so much public as the Sartrean "practico-inerts": these passive spaces envelop us as lifeless backdrop, a bit like dead labor functions in redundant fixed capital, in plain-old bricks and mortar, in a concrete and steel that imprisons. On the other hand, for urban spaces to come alive, to be public in Rousseau's republican sense (not the Tea Party's), they need to express dynamic social relations between people, between people there and elsewhere, elsewhere in other urban spaces, bringing those spaces to life as well, creating a network of living, conjoined, organic spaces—sovereign spaces, we might say—not dead zones that alienate and separate.

Thus people in these sovereign spaces might come together to *create* a function, to talk and meet, to hang out. Sometimes they'll come to protest, to express themselves in angry not tender ways. In either sense, they're not responding to a function like a crowd of shoppers. In coming together they'll express active rather than passive affects; plazas, parks, squares, streets and civic buildings thereby become what Jeffrey Hou calls, in a contribution to the collection

Beyond Zuccotti Park, "insurgent public space." "[A]s we envision the future of public space in North America and beyond," Hou says, "it is clear that the focus of our efforts should be equally, if not more, on the making of the public than on the making of space. While space remains critical as a vehicle for actions and expressions, it is through the actions and the making of a socially and politically engaged public that the struggle for public space as a forum of political dialogues and expressions can be resuscitated and sustained."[5]

Following Rousseau, the "incorruptible" Robespierre insisted that the poor have most need of ensuring their voice gets *heard*, that their needs take priority in any remaking of the public realm. But to speak out, in the making of a public of the kind that Hou articulates, there is a need, among other things, for a free press, for an alternative free press, a press open and publicly accessible, a press that reports on the sort of news items people *ought* to hear about. This is not the celebrity gossip and right-wing propaganda mainstream media booms out every day, at every hour, the fear and loathing peddled by the likes of Fox and News International, but of other sources, often online media, sometimes clandestine media. If a space to petition guarantees a citizen's right to be heard, then a free press guarantees a citizen's right to *hear*, to *listen* to genuine social truths getting circulated within the *cité*. To speak and to hear correspondingly require an urban space in which to debate and argue, and, above all, to meet, some place where citizens can come together. Robespierre acknowledged the need for democracy to allow people to assemble, to do so peaceably and without arms; although, of course, if this "right" is denied, if the principles of free assembly are opposed, then the sub-clause is that citizens ought to be able to assemble through any means necessary, peaceable or otherwise. It is in this space that citizens have the power to *act*, to act after being *heard*, to act after having *listened* to other citizens; mutually reinforcing public agoras—citizens' agora—as much experiential spaces as physical locations.

The dilemma here, however, is that the citizens' agora is needed both sides of the urban insurrection: on the one hand, it's required

5. Jeffrey Hou, "Making Public, Beyond Public Space," in Ron Shiffman et al., eds, *Beyond Zuccotti Park*, New Village Press, Oakland CA, 2012, p. 94.

to initially put in place a revolutionary insurrection, is instrumental, in other words, in the insurrection itself, for propagandizing and organizing the insurrection, for spreading the word and for news sharing—even if, sometimes, this organization initially needs to be discreet, needs to tread cautiously in its propagation of open democracy. New social media can obviously be one component for creating a new citizen's agora, for listening to news of what's important, as well as for voicing what any aspiring general will needs to hear. On the other hand, the day after the insurrection such an agora needs to be inscribed into a written constitution, into an actual urban social contract guaranteeing they remain the rights of all citizens.

In a way, Rousseau's *Social Contract* seems better attuned to the post-insurrectional epoch, to the aftermath of citizens' revolutionary upheaval, to the day after the big event, when the urban carnivals are over, when the insurrection has triumphed, if it ever triumphs; "rights-talk" beforehand isn't maybe the best means through which to gain one's rights. In fact, one might wonder whether the whole theme of "rights"—rights of man, right to the city (*le droit à la ville*), etc.—really helps; rights-talk can sometimes inhibit rather than enable things to happen. Rights can be positive and negative depending on how you swing, depending on how you frame them politically: they are *empty signifiers* that need filling with content, and once you've filled them their implications are so indeterminate that opposing parties can use the same rights language to express absolutely differing positions.

Le droit à la ville is an unfortunate victim. At the United Nations-sponsored "World Urban Forum," held in Rio in March 2010, the UN and the World Bank both incorporated "the right to the city" into its charter to address the global poverty trap. On the other side of the street in Rio, at the "Urban Social Forum," a people's popular alternative was also being staged; there activists were appalled by the ruling class's re-appropriation of such a hallowed grassroots ideal, of its right not *theirs*. The mainstream has now converted its own right into a tactical right that's often become a watchword for conservative rule. The Tories in Britain are quick to acknowledge peoples' right to self-management, happily endorsing "community rights" and "citizens' right to choose," since all this means the neoliberal state can now desist from coughing up for public services. Self-empowerment thereby becomes tantamount to self-subsidization, to self-exploitation, to even more dispossession, mollified as "social enterprise" and the voluntary "third sector."

So rights, including the right to the city, have no catch-all universal meaning in politics, nor any foundational basis in institutions; neither are they responsive to any moral or legal argument: questions of rights are, first and foremost, questions of *social power*, about who *wins*. The struggle for rights isn't something "recognized" by some higher, neutral arbiter. Instead, for those people who have no rights, rights to the *cité* must be taken. They involve struggle and force, a fight, sometimes to the death, this side of the insurrection. What has been taken must be reclaimed, by force, reclaimed through practical action, through organized militancy, though urban insurrection. A Bill of Rights remains the ends not the means for enforcing one's democratic right. It's the joyous product not the guiding light in the dogged process of struggle.

* * *

Twenty-first-century neo-Haussmannization not only upgrades and intensifies the contradictions of nineteenth-century Haussmannization, it equally, and ironically, upgrades and intensifies the possibilities for expanding the citizens' agora—for providing both the means and the ends for such an agora. In *All That is Solid Melts into Air*, Marshall Berman took Baudelaire under his wing to illustrate how Haussmann's boulevards prized open a modern form of urban publicity. "The new Parisian boulevard." Berman says, "was the most spectacular innovation of the nineteenth-century, and the decisive breakthrough in the modernization of the traditional city."[6] The boulevards wreaked devastating destruction, smashed through whole neighborhoods that had lived and evolved, tight-knitted, for centuries. Afterwards, though, for the first time ever, the whole city

6. Marshall Berman, *All That is Solid Melts into Air*, Verso, London, 1988, p. 150.

was open to its inhabitants. "After centuries of life as a cluster of isolated cells," Berman says (p. 151), "Paris was becoming a unified physical and human space."

For Berman, Baudelaire's Paris Spleen poem "The Eyes of the Poor" vividly shows what this new kind of extroverted urbanization can do to private bodies in public space (and to public bodies in private space). Two young lovers sit near the window of a dazzling new café, lining one of Haussmann's newly-minted boulevards. They dreamily look at each other. They're inside, sharing one another's company, admiring one another, yet they're able to survey through the window the gaiety outside, the street activity, the delightful bustle of *la nouvelle vie parisienne*. After a while, a ragged homeless family passes by. Enamored by the café's garish opulence, they stop. They peer in; the kids press their noses against the gleaming windowpane, admiring the decor and people inside. "How beautiful it is!" Baudelaire has his ragpickers explain. "How beautiful it is!" But they know it's not for them, not for their type. Yet their fascination, Berman says (p. 149), "carries no hostile undertones; their vision of the gulf between the two worlds is sorrowful, not militant, not resentful but resigned." (Collective resentment would culminate only a decade or so later in the Commune.) The male lover is touched by this "family of eyes" outside; he feels a strange kinship with them, a strange affinity, despite the social distance. His lover is unmoved; she wants the patron to shoo them away, to move them on, somewhere else, anywhere so long as it's out of *her* sight. "These people with their great saucer eyes," Baudelaire has her declaim, "are unbearable!" At that moment the two lovers love each other a little less.

Haussmann's urban reality is romantic and magical; private joys spring from wide-open public spaces. One can henceforth be private in the crowd, alone yet amidst people; one can be inside while outside, outside while inside. There are walls *and* there is transparency. There is social closure *and* physical openness. There is public invisibility *and* private visibility. Berman says that Baudelaire's "Eyes of the Poor" poem evokes a "primal scene," a primal scene "that reveals some of the deepest ironies and contradictions" of modern capitalist urbanization. It's the "and" that expresses the duplicity; the coexistence between apparently contradictory realities isn't a "but"

but an "and." They go together, inextricably. For Berman (p. 153), the setting that now

> makes all urban humanity a great extended "family of eyes" also brings forth the discarded stepchildren of that family. The physical and social transformations that drove the poor out of sight now bring them back directly into everyone's line of vision. Haussmann, in tearing down the old medieval slums, inadvertently broke down the self-enclosed and hermetically sealed world of traditional urban poverty. The boulevards, blasting great holes though the poorest neighborhoods, enable the poor to walk through the holes and out of their ravaged neighborhoods, to discover for the first time what the rest of their city and the rest of life are like.

They are but one step away from asserting themselves as citizens, citizens of a wider universe, citizens expressing adequate ideas about all kinds of common notions they're now capable of developing. They're one step away from developing a citizens' agora.

Fast-forward a century and a half. Neo-Haussmannization is a strategy that has likewise blasted open millions of neighborhoods the planet over. Now, the Baudelairean "family of eyes" has gone truly global. Those "great saucer eyes" are media eyes, all seeing, and, with the Internet and WikiLeaks, often all-knowing too, or potentially all-knowing. People can now see the global aristocratic elite along this planetary information and communication boulevard, see them through the windowpanes of neoliberal global-urban life. We might even say that a global family of eyes has the potentiality to encounter itself as a family, as an emerging citizenry, as an affinity group that yearns to repossess what has been dispossessed. Their big saucer eyes now look on with indignation, in a citizens' agora currently making itself, doing so with animosity as well as awe. Now, there's not so much a world for the working class to win as a whole world for urban citizens to occupy, to reclaim and remake as their *cité*.

9

Taking Back Urban Politics

Neutrality isn't cool.

—Justin Ravitz, Marxist Judge of Detroit Recorder's Court, 1980

A little while ago, I participated in an evening of revolutionary urban politics at the Roxy Bar and Screen, an independent arts cinema and hip drinking den near London Bridge. Hosted by University College London's "Urban Laboratory" (under Ben Campkin's direction) and compered by Louis Moreno (who also provided the Detroit techno groove), a packed young crowd settled into watching two rare documentaries from 1970 and 1980: *Finally Got the News* and *Taking Back Detroit*. "Revolutionary urban politics," I know, might sound hyperbolic, even pretentious; but the two films really were about doing something militantly radical, about folks from the past organizing themselves to kick up a fuss and fight the power. Indeed, the energy of the two films created a charge that night, kindled the audience, and prompted everybody to think about what being revolutionary might still mean today, about what doing the right thing might still entail.[1]

1. *Finally Got the News* and *Taking Back Detroit* are both available from Icarus Films in Brooklyn, New York: www.icarusfilms.com/new2003/fin.html and www.icarusfilms.com/cat97/t-z/taking_b.html. The playing of these films at the Roxy Bar and Screen didn't emerge out of a political vacuum, but grew out of the Moreno's "Spatial Fix" reading group, which had met in London for a number of weeks prior, reading and debating Dan Georgakas and Marvin Survin's great book on Detroit from 1975, *Detroit: I Do Mind Dying* (Redwords, London, 1999). Just as reading groups, like filmmaking, assumed great political significance for participants in the two documentaries on show, they can still help disseminate radical ideas and offer correctives to contaminating bourgeois propaganda.

Finally Got the News hits out in hard-edged black and white; apt because it is about hard-edged black and white: Steward Bird, Rene Lichtman and Peter Gessner tell the tale of the League of Revolutionary Black Workers, an umbrella organization uniting Revolutionary Union Movements at Detroit's auto plants in the late 1960s. The aesthetic smacks of *nouvelle vague* montage, with hints of Eisenstein thrown in; but the atmosphere is of direct, head-on confrontation. Images of lynchings are overlaid with booming African tribal drums; rage wafts menacingly in the air, like in Miles Davis's *Bitches Brew*, which figures in the film; Miles's electrified trumpet rings out like a hammer knocking, getting inside your head, hard to ignore, a screaming comes across the sky. The film's dialogue is black-cat and wild-cat, picketing and angry, like DRUM (Dodge Revolutionary Union Movement) organizer John Watson's opening tirade, denouncing, Marxist-Leninist-style, the blatant exploitation at Chrysler's Eldon Avenue Gear and Axle plant, about the super-profits and surplus value gleaned from its black workforce; about assembly-line speed-ups, floridly labeled "niggermation" by black employees; about on-the-job harassment by foremen; about industrial illnesses and death; about black workers feeling let down by the United Auto Workers union (UAW), sucking up to corporate bosses, too concerned with their reputation, with their own bureaucratic self-reproduction, to be bothered about affecting any real change.

Early on in *Finally Got the News*, in the frozen dawn darkness, two shift workers journey along an empty expressway, listening to Joe Carter's blues song on the radio: "Please, Mr. Foreman, slow down your assembly line / I said, Lord, why don't you slow down that assembly line? / No, I don't mind workin', but I do mind dyin'."[2] In Detroit, it's said, people don't just sing the blues, they literally live the blues everyday. Blues can mean resigned passivity, an acceptance of one's poor lot, yet sometimes blues can prompt engaged activity, even

2. The refrain, written by a Ford Rouge production-line worker, would of course inspire Dan Georgakas and Marvin Surkin's book on the League, *Detroit, I Do Mind Dying: A Study in Urban Revolution* (St. Martin's Press, New York, 1975).

interventionist action, a raging sense that enough's enough, already; this shit must stop right here.

Still, rage can move in a number of directions: It can be eruptive and destructive, like it was in July 1967, when, after the cops raided a poor after-hours bar, a "Blind Pig," altercations outside between its African-American patrons and the police sparked one of the worst public disturbances in US history. After almost a week of looting and tense, violent confrontations with the police, and after President Johnson sent in the National Guard and Army (together with tanks), 43 people lay dead, 2,500 properties were destroyed, and over 7,000 people had gotten arrested. For black Detroiters this wasn't a riot but the *Great Rebellion*, a rebellion against years and years of institutional and popular racism and discrimination: "Burn Baby Burn!" was their mantra.

The rage glimpsed in *Finally Got the News* is, however, another kind of rage that organized and channeled itself collectively, that aimed itself at a common enemy, that waged and raged against the structures of white corporate and state power. This is a *dignified rage*, a *class rage*, expressing an anger that just about keeps itself in check. Ken Cockrel, a lawyer and a Central Staff member of the League, a prime-mover in defending workers' rights in the courtroom, takes this rage close to the nihilistic edge. Those soft "executives" working at their desks, he says, going to Harvard, to Yale and Wharton School of Business, never producing anything, never really doing anything:

> they're mother-fucking, non-producing, non-existing bastards dealing with paper. They give you little bullshit amounts of money—wages and so forth—and then they steal that shit back from you in terms of the way they have their other thing set up, that old credit-stick-'em up gimmick society. . . It's these mother-fuckers who deal with intangibles who are rewarded by society... this whole mother-fucking society is controlled by this little clique which is parasitic, vulturistic and cannibalistic and is sucking and destroying the life of workers everywhere; and we must stop it![3]

3. Cockerel's rap is cited in Georgakas and Surkin, *Detroit, I Do Mind Dying*, p. 131.

It was such rage that fueled *organized* and *disciplined* revolutionary practice, a form of rebellion made by black people in a white man's world, a world that less than 100 years ago still had the institution of slavery. To be black in the United States means, as Frantz Fanon put it in *The Wretched of the Earth*, to possess a "Third World state of mind," "an ancestral pride strangely resembling defiance," a defiance the League expressed; a growing radicalization of African-Americans in the second half of the twentieth century, shifting from the rural Southern plantation states toward the northern and midwestern industrialized plantation states, toward the urban ghettos, with a new emphasis on economic injustice and police brutality, of getting hassled at the plant as well as on the street.

Finally Got the News was made a year before the League of Black Revolutionary Workers folded, as much because of internal tensions as external pressure. In the documentary, we don't get to hear an epitaph about its ripping apart. However, as the League's grip loosened in the factories, it found itself getting displaced into another political arena, into the nitty-gritty legal realm, into electoral politics, infiltrating the courts and challenging the civil system, re-appropriating it for the little guys, trying to create a bigger urban space for worker organization and community coalitions. Cockrel and his law firm partner, Justin Ravitz, the "Marxist judge," began to build and use the black worker base of the League to bid for elective office. Control of the factories and control of the streets, they felt, needed to go hand in hand with control of the courts and the cops. Rebellion could and should be waged on three fronts: at the workplace, in the courts, and out in the community.

* * *

By the late 1970s, around 1980, when *Taking Back Detroit* was made, Ravitz and Cockrel had both entered public office; the former was elected to a ten-year stint as judge of "Recorder's Court," the latter to a seat on Detroit's City Council. Now, Motor City no longer appears in harsh cinematic and racial black and white; we see it instead through the lenses of softer-toned color. The imagery isn't entirely coincidental, for now, too, the modus operandi had changed, to the degree that elective office became the base for building a city-wide political movement. Now, the drama isn't so much about *direct confrontation* as *pragmatic engagement*. The rage is calmer, older, maybe more mature: but rage there still is. The fire this time burned not from outside but inside the power structure, inside the courtroom and at City Hall; and *Taking Back Detroit* takes us patiently behind the scenes, into the committee rooms and council chambers, down tense courthouse corridors—Michigan law forbids actual filming in court—into the endless meetings and strategizing luncheons.

Ravitz and Cockrel and their fellow-traveler brothers and sisters (like ace organizer Sheila Murphy, Cockrel's wife) earned reputations as crusaders for working and poor black and white people, winning high-profile lawsuits, putting the establishment on trial—the judiciary, the corporation, and the police. Cockrel rallied as an "independent Marxist," speaking out against black mayor Coleman Young's courting of the business community; and against the business community pulling the strings of its marionette mayor. Cockrel became famous and infamous (depending on your political persuasion) for his brilliant intellect and rapid-fire tongue; an eloquence that could dazzle audiences, that grudgingly gained respect even from adversaries. (Watch him in *Taking Back Detroit* at a public hearing on neighborhood revitalization, slickly dealing with GM's clumsy honky henchmen.) Ravitz, meanwhile, became the people's judge who didn't wear a robe, who successfully defends welfare mothers and anti-war demonstrators; the calm, slowly-speaking Ravitz also broke protocol: in his courtroom Law and Order, the judge (himself) and the spectators had to stand up for the entering jury (not vice versa).

"Taking back the city" (rather than the factory) became the new radical clarion call, 1980s-style. The worker base was there, still, just about, but with greatly reduced level of militancy. For a while, an African-American workforce was indispensable for a particular epoch of American industrialization, an epoch that's been labeled "Fordist." Yet from being indispensable it turned out that they were only a contingent workforce all along. Now, a "post-Fordist," "post-industrial" epoch of capitalism no longer needed them, had "set them free" from the immediate process of production, as Marx said. In Detroit, the factories began folding or relocating overseas where labor costs are cheaper (auto plants uprooted to Mexico); offices and infrastructure got abandoned; white populations fled in droves to the suburbs; the city's tax base shrank; ruins ran by the block rather than by building; and violent crime soared. Between 1950 and 1980, Detroit lost nearly 50 percent of its manufacturing jobs and a staggering 1 million of its population. Corporate capital had literally abandoned the city, walked away from it, in a familiar, though dramatically intensified story of what was then happening everywhere to urban America. The structures of white corporate power once created a particular city through its own *presence*, through its own industrial image; now, its *absence* continued to shape the urban fabric, tore it to tatters.

Nostrums began to enter the federal discourse, aimed at addressing fiscal crisis. One, by Daniel Patrick Moynihan (Nixon's urban affairs advisor), stemming from 1969, was "Benign Neglect." Nothing "benign" here, though, since this was the *purposeful* running down of blighted neighborhoods, henceforth seen as no longer economically "viable," too much of a federal burden to fix; "Malign Neglect" opponents called it, emphasizing the "active" pathological nature of the process. Its partner in urban crime at the time was "Planned Shrinkage," the Manhattan Institute's Roger Starr's brainchild, which federally "planned" the elimination of "bad" (read: poor, minority) neighborhoods across America. The paradigmatic case-study of Planned Shrinkage was New York's South Bronx—it was too expensive for fire stations and fire trucks to keep putting out all those fires!—but black inner city neighborhoods of Detroit suffered appallingly as targets of extinction, too. In 1984, Marshall Berman called these crimes against urban humanity "urbicide": the murder of the city. Despite the body count, his verdict never led to any arrests.[4]

---

4. Marshall Berman, "Roots, Ruins, Renewals: City Life After Urbicide," *Village Voice*, September 4, 1984. Actually, the term "urbicide" dates back to an earlier generation, coined by the architectural critic Ada Louise Huxtable in her *Will They Ever Finish Bruckner Boulevard? A Primer on Urbicide* (Collier Books, New York, 1963). The text is a passionate assault—done by a passionate carer—on an urban planning and renewal establishment who seemed not to care and who practiced "death by development." Huxtable lays into architectural and urban renewal follies like the Lincoln Center

But then a curious thing happened: at the backend of the 1970s, and as the 1980s kicked in, federal government changed tack. Crying poverty only a few years earlier, announcing its inability to sustain demand-oriented collective consumption proclivities, government came up with the idea that federal money should try to leverage private capital investment, entice it back into urban areas previously shunned or abandoned. Before long, the private sector could bag all kinds of tax abatements, rent holidays and federal grants: CDBGs and UDAGs were two popular acronyms, Community Development Block Grants and Urban Development Action Grants (inventions of the Carter administration in 1977), interest-free sponsorship when interest rates for ordinary people were enormously high.

Notwithstanding the federal mandate that CDBGs should fund low- and moderate-income people, federal public dollars poured into Detroit's riverfront development, whose crowning glory became the "Renaissance Center" and John Portman's 73-storey Marriott hotel. Public dollars flooded into upscale redevelopment and proved a bonanza for private investors. Critics grumbled that all this hastened, not ameliorated, social polarization and inequality; few of the goodies ever seemed to trickle down to needy people. UDAGs sponsored convention centers, hotels, marinas, and expensive residential complexes and became the greatest hotel-building venture in American history. And if that wasn't enough, these hotels barely paid employees minimum wage; chains like Hyatt and Marriott also turned into big time union busters.

In the 1980s, the City of Detroit passed hundreds of project abatements of real estate and property taxes, freely giving away land, granting interest-free loans and federal monies *with no strings attached*, other than the investors stay around a while, which often they didn't. Cockrel pushed for *quid pro quos*, maintaining that part of the deal should be for recipients to guarantee a certain number of jobs and commit themselves for *x* number of years. The line didn't go down well in council. In one revealing scene from *Taking Back*

---

and World Trade Center, as well as the Bruckner expressway, which hacked through the South Bronx. "In New York," writes Huxtable, "neighborhoods fall like dominoes."

Detroit, Mayor Young leads a tax abatement debate. "Yes, Yes, Yes, Yes . . . ," goes the vote, as every councilor agrees to the deal, until Cockrel, defiantly, says "No." He's the sole nay—the sole brother with soul.

Some of the most fascinating sequences of Stephen Lighthill's marvelous documentary—aspects that make it an uplifting, inspiring vision of Detroit when it could've easily been depressing—are when Cockrel and Ravitz recognize their constituency isn't inside City Hall: it's ordinary folks on the outside, in the redlined and block-busted neighborhoods. If Cockrel is dead against tax abatements for capital, he's categorically *for* something else; he dares for DARE: Detroit Alliance for a Rational Economy, a different vision of another Detroit, a bottom-up vision of outsiders helping insiders reshape that inside. On film, we witness DARE campaigners and activists running teach-in bus tours around Detroit's new waterfront, letting ordinary people, hitherto excluded from decision-making, hear and vividly see for themselves where their tax dollars and public monies go: into the upscale construction right outside the bus window.

It's an amazing propagandizing outfit Cockrel and Murphy orchestrate, exposing the ruling class's political-economic shenanigans, revealing its behind-closed-door deals and machinations, stuff that people *should* know about. DARE dared to mobilize Detroit's residents, dared to be mobilized by Detroit's residents, and tried in the mix to get community control of basic urban institutions back on the public agenda. Maybe the only thing that had really changed in Cockrel's politicking since the League of Revolutionary Black Workers glory days was the battlefield: "the primary thing that can be done to prevent the occurrence of repression," he told an audience on January 30, 1970 at Detroit's Saint Joseph's Church, "is for those of us of the oppressed classes to take over, to take power, to run every goddamn thing in this country, to run everything, this world—and certainly to start out by running everything in this city."[5]

* * *

5. Ken Cockerel, "From Repression to Revolution," speech downloadable at http://libcom.org/library/repression-revolution-speech-kenneth-v-cockrel

It's sad and touching to think that Cockrel's life was suddenly cut short not long after *Taking Back Detroit*: he died, after a massive heart attack, in 1989, aged 50. By that point, disillusioned with disempowered insiderness, he'd decided not to stand for re-election. He went back to practicing law, rejoining old partner Ravitz, and began considering running for real power, for the Mayor of Detroit, a longstanding dream, until that fateful April 25th day struck him down and out. What to add about these two films that isn't self-evident from viewing them? What could I say in my after-film rap, late in the night, to a boozy audience, the majority of whom weren't even born when *Taking Back Detroit* first aired? What political message could be gleaned, continues to speak to younger generations *now*, still resonates as we hear news of Detroit's bankruptcy, circa 2013/4?

The city teeters on edge of collapse with a $900 million budget shortfall for 2012 (and $18 billion in long-term liability). (How much of this debacle, I wonder, is rooted in the 1980s? When precious tax dollars weren't invested in public infrastructure, but handed out to the private sector, who duly pocketed the booty and later split the scene.) Incumbent Mayor David Bing has relinquished power to Kevyn Orr, the "emergency financial manager," who in 2009 helped (along with a federal bale out) Chrysler resolve its Chapter 11 woes. (Over the years, federal government has bailed out all Detroit's auto industry.) Now, apparently, "everything is on the table," says Orr. Which means more public sector layoffs, more selling off of public assets, further privatization of city services, including, to belt-tighten utilities, dimmer (and darkened) streets at night. Diego Rivera's great frescos at the Detroit Art Institute would doubtless fetch a tidy sum at private auction, too. There's an idea! R.I.P. Ken Cockrel . . .

As at November 2013, the City appears set to file for Chapter 9 bankruptcy, which would fend off creditors and release federal aid. But it's a devil's bargain since it necessitates slashing public employee pensions and other severe municipal austerity measures; unions and retiree groups have denounced the bankruptcy plan (and its consequences) as unlawful. The courts stand ready to make a legal decision. Meanwhile, an effort is underway to ditch Orr after he made controversial comments about the people he's supposed to be helping. A petition drive calls on the emergency manager to step down over his comments, made in the *Wall Street Journal* (August 2, 2013), describing Detroiters as "dumb, lazy, happy and rich." Wendell Anthony, President of Detroit's National Association for the Advancement of Colored People (NAACP), said despite Orr's subsequent apology, the petition drive continues. "We won't be insulted and demeaned by the self-proclaimed 'benevolent dictator'," the petition says, referring to Orr. Anthony also points the finger at Michigan state governor Rick Snyder. "[Snyder] is responsible. He is the one who put Detroit and the surrounding communities in this position after 2.3 million Michiganders said no, they did not want this process, lest we forget. And so," Anthony said, "what we have is a situation where now, chickens are coming home to roost in terms of how can you represent me if you don't really respect me."

On the podium at the Roxy Bar and Screen, I remind people of *Do the Right Thing*, a film made the same year as Cockrel's death, another tale of tense race-relations and urban politics. I recall the moment when Radio Raheem goes into Sal's Bed-Stuy pizzeria with his boom-box blazing Public Enemy's *Fight the Power*. Radio Raheem won't turn the volume down; Sal gets mad and loses his rag, reaches for his baseball bat, and, bawling assorted racial epithets, smashes the boom-box to smithereens. (Sal seemed like a decent, tolerant guy, an honest Italian-American serving a modest-means black clientele, but really he's a racist like a lot of them.) Radio Raheem leaps across the counter, onto Sal, and a fight erupts. Black customers pitch in, wrecking chairs and ripping Frank Sinatra, Al Pacino, Joe DiMaggio, Robert De Niro et al. off the pizzeria's Wall of Fame (Buggin' Out had always complained there weren't any *brothers* on that wall). The police, with sirens blazing, step in and in the tussle kill Raheem. Locals arrive, including Mookie, Sal's delivery boy (played by director Spike Lee), to see what's going down. They recognize the police brutality, the racism, the lack of respect. Then we watch Mookie walk away, think he's leaving, that tensions have calmed and it's time for everyone to go home. But suddenly Mookie picks up a garbage can, turns around, and, running back into the fray, hurls it through Sal's windowpane. All hell breaks loose, an insurrectional moment, a *rebellion*, a ransacking of Sal's place. (The long history of urban "riots" has shown us how destruction and property damage is rarely indiscriminate. During the 1981 uprisings in my native Liverpool, two of the first targets to go up in smoke in Toxteth were the Racquet Club, a rich, white-gents-only establishment, and the Rialto dancehall, which for years barred blacks.)

This window-breaking act, the most significant in the film, didn't do Mookie a whole lot of good. He lost his job and his employer, lost a steady bit of income. Yet *he did the right thing*. He knew something wasn't quite right. He knew there was injustice going down, that Sal was really a racist. What we saw tonight, I say, with those guys from the League, with Cockrel and Ravitz, were people who, maybe above all else, also *did the right thing*. The League knew there was injustice at the plant, knew workers were being ripped off, exploited, dehumanized. So they organized, they did the right thing against the union and the bosses. The thing about doing the right thing is that, often, your actions are conditioned by a basic principle of what's just and what's unjust, about what's fair and unfair. And there's a limit to which you can be pushed around before something gives, before something begins to intrude on those principles, violates those principles. This can get you into a lot of trouble. We saw it in *Taking Back Detroit*, when in the council chambers, Ken Cockrel was the only no vote, saying no when everybody else said yes.

Here's a guy who acted on principle, who wanted to do the right thing. It didn't go down well with his fellow councilors, nor with Mr. Mayor Young. If we fast forward 30-odd years, if we saw this same city office today, or any city office, any formal meeting in a bureaucracy—and we have bureaucracies everywhere in our lives today, don't we; some of us likely participate in them—as a vote gets cast, what would happen? My bet is that what you really think, according to the principles of your value system, is, like Cockrel, NO, that doing the right thing necessitates a NO vote. And yet, when the hands eventually go up, somehow you vote YES alongside everybody else. Afterwards, quietly and privately, perhaps under your own breath, perhaps whispering to somebody else, off-record, you admit you really didn't agree with a YES, but you thought it best to comply, to follow the majority. (And who knows whether others thought like you?)

In a sense, I think this explains much about what has happened since 1980, what we glimpse here in *Taking Back Detroit*. That is how doing the right thing, how having a principled value system, has been whittled away in ways that people—us—really weren't aware of. We have somehow sold ourselves out. We waved the white flag of conciliatory surrender long ago, began to participate in what Guy Debord, in 1988 (in *Comments on The Society of the Spectacle*), called "the mass psychology of submission." By not saying NO, by not taking a defiant stand, we eventually created a world with a self-perpetuating feeling of frustration about what can and cannot be done, about what we can and cannot achieve. As it stands today, submission has consolidated itself into a self-reinforcing notion that real change is no longer possible, so why even bother to try; and so those principles of doing the right thing, at first slowly, then steady, now rapidly, are tossed out of the committee meeting room, out of sight and out of mind.

Nowadays, there are many decent, honest people who maybe haven't so much sold out on their principles, but who find it hard to relocate those principles, to aim those principles, and to have the courage to act upon those principles. Those guys on film didn't sell out on their principles, neither as outsiders in the League nor as insiders in City Hall. They did the right thing as both outsiders and insiders; and in doing the right thing as insiders, which is perhaps the hardest place of all to act on principle, people like Ravitz and Cockrel became a species that anyone who's still interested in revolutionary politics, who still might even believe in revolutionary politics, needs to become: a *double agent*. We have to know the law, know how to "play" the game on an unimportant pragmatic level; but at the deeper level of values, of values that you hold dear to your heart, values that are non-negotiable and which inspire your hope and optimism—they must guide your important actions. The trick is figuring out how you can find other people who feel the same, who share the same value system, who admit it out loud, and how you can act together around those principles.

And like folks in *Finally Got the News* and *Taking Back Detroit*, there are lots of us around who, on principle, have had enough with what's going down these days, had enough with governments' ubiquitous austerity programs; we're sick to death with calls for public sector downsizing and private sector rightsizing. This as Wall Street fat cats get fatter and fatter; this as on Budget Day in 2013, when Chancellor George Osborne implores ordinary Britons to continue the squeeze, Barclays' bigwigs pocket shares worth £40 million. (Investment banker Rich Ricci didn't dally in cashing in his £17.6 million's worth.)

Now the arena of battle isn't just about the workplace, nor even about the city: it's about the globe, about urban society. And if we factor in social media, this means we can organize and communicate with our soul brothers and sisters thousands of miles away, see their faces on Facebook, share stories about oppression and injustice, about corporate lies and governmental blind-eyes, do it with Egyptians and Tunisians, with Turks and Greeks and Spanish *Indignados*, with occupiers and workers, with insiders and outsiders everywhere. We can try to do the right thing together; say NO when politicians and bankers say YES, say YES when they say NO.

It's time to take back the world, to channel our seething rage about those mother-fucking intangibles, time to organize our own counter-propaganda machine; make films like the League did, start newspapers, inform the people and reform things now, see ourselves as part of moving history, as history lived as ongoing struggle, as a process wherein we're the subject who's *finally getting the news*. The key militant tagline we might hold dear is one Ken Cockrel knew well: DARE: dare to challenge, dare to fight the power, dare to OCCUPY, dare to confront the structures of power and wealth that are only entrenched because we've let them be entrenched. Dare to do the right thing. Those who fight can lose, Bertolt Brecht famously said; but those who don't fight have already lost.

10

Whose City? The Parasites', of course . . .

In 1970, the English sociologist Ray Pahl published a collection of essays under a simple yet disarming title, *Whose City?*. The question was more original than it sounded, even if its answer was fairly obvious; and Pahl knew it: "One doesn't have to be very astute now," he said in an introduction to the second edition of the text, "in order to answer the question 'Whose City?': quite evidently the capitalists own British cities and up to 1973 they grew fat on their rents and the revaluations of their portfolios."[1] What interested Pahl and other critical urban scholars of that era—many of whom like Pahl and Manuel Castells went on to create the *International Journal of Urban and Regional Research* (in 1977)—was how come it was *their* city and not *ours*? What were the mechanisms whereby capitalists—increasingly finance capitalists—commandeered the city in the way they did? Through what means did they make it their city? How did planning authorities, land-use allocations, and various state agencies perpetuate or undermine this "system"? The bold originality of the thinking then was that it did indeed identify a "system," an "urban system," a class system through which fat cats grew rich. There was, still is, a logic at play, with structures and institutions that enabled, still enable, this logic to function, to reproduce itself systemically. "The city," wrote Pahl (p. 194), with typical blunt insight, "is what society lets it be." The dialectic between the city and society would never be the same again.

The approach Ray Pahl pioneered quickly became known as "urban managerialism." This for a number of reasons, both analytical

1. Ray Pahl, *Whose City?*, Penguin Books, Harmondsworth, 1970, p. 1.

and political. First off is that, analytically, "the system" has its human embodiment, which is to say, has active players who make decisions even while they constrain themselves by the decisions they make. Pahl suggested that there were a host of "urban managers" who effect the life chances of ordinary people in decisive and uneven ways; they effect life chances because these managers have a certain authority and relative autonomy in the allocation of "scarce" urban resources, the most precious of which is housing. By urban managers, Pahl meant housing officers, planners, social workers and decision-making bureaucrats, those employed by state authorities, housing associations and local municipalities, those who acted, both wittingly or unwittingly, as "social gatekeepers." To analyze how these urban managers acted, to identify empirically their common ideology (if they had one), the actual allocative decisions and manipulations they made, and why, was, said Pahl, a legitimate object of enquiry for socially committed sociologists. The allocative mechanism, in other words, "how much of the cake and for whom?," how this created "territorial inequalities," how it affected the sort of schools children went to, as well as access to other public resources like hospitals and mass transit, became, for Pahl, a focus of intense *political* concern.

While Pahl, like many progressive urbanists of that generation, was influenced by Marxism, by a critical analysis of capitalist urban political-economy, the politics of *Whose City?* might be best described as left Weberian. Unlike Castells and David Harvey, as a social democrat believing in redistributive justice and a benevolent, welfare capitalist state, Pahl balked at throwing in his lot with Marxism *tout court*. He was always more interested in collective consumption rather than productive consumption; and his emphasis on Max Weber's trinity of "wealth, status, and power" meant a class analysis that scrutinized urban space and resource allocation rather than work relations as such.[2] His fundamental concern was what does

2. In later work, like his study of informality on Kent's Isle of Sheppey (see *Divisions of Labour*, Basil Blackwell, Oxford, 1984), Pahl rethought the nature of work. He began to see it as something much more than simply what happened at the workplace. Work incorporated home and community, too; production and reproduction are but different facets of mutually constituted phenomena.

class mean in an urbanizing context, and here he only dabbled with Weberian thinking, never going the whole hog like Peter Saunders and Peter Williams et al., for whom "consumption classes" won out over production classes.[3]

At the time, David Harvey seemed to be countering Pahl when he claimed that urban struggles represented "displaced" class struggles, struggles condensed from workplace struggles; although, more recently, Harvey says struggles in the urban arena are no longer displaced, given restructuring of capitalist work relations and the denigration of unionization. Urban struggles, on the contrary, represent the most intense and amplified of class struggles: the arena of the social factory has now enlarged onto the whole productive plane of city itself.[4] But Harvey explained to me in an email exchange that "Pahl found his own answer in his Sheppey study, which I am now happy to accept."[5] "I used the idea of displaced class struggle," Harvey said

> not as an antidote to Ray's anti-Marxism; it's more to deal with what I now refer to as the distinction between the production and realization of surplus value in urban settings, because all along I could see that as much value was being extracted by the property owners and rentiers (with the aid of urban managerialists) as by direct producers at the point of production. I always felt close to Ray in terms of his identification of the urban question even as I pulled in different directions for answers (he made very little of urban rent, for example, which I emphasized and would still emphasize).

In subsequent renderings of his managerialist thesis, Pahl responded positively to comradely Marxist criticism like this. "By

3. P. Saunders and P. Williams (1986) "The New Conservatism: Some Thoughts on Recent and Future Developments in Urban Studies," *Environment and Planning D: Society and Space*, Volume 4: 393–9; and P. Saunders and P. Williams (1987) "Reconsidering Social Theory: A Debate," *Environment and Planning D: Society and Space*, Volume 5: 427–34.
4. David Harvey, *Rebel Cities: From the Right to the City to the Urban Revolution*, Verso, London, 2012.
5. Email of June 11, 2013. Cf. Harvey, *Rebel Cities*, p. 179, n. 5.

focusing on urban resources and facilities," he admitted, with his own emphases, "and by alerting urban populations to their relative deprivations in the field of consumption, attention is shifted from the main *source* of inequality, namely, the field of production." "If workers are made to think that *their main interests* are in the field of consumption, and if sociologists adopt a form of urban managerialism to explain the allocation of resources within an urban system, then clearly basic inequalities arising from the productive process may remain hidden."[6]

* * *

When I first read Ray Pahl's *Whose City?* in the 1980s I was a 20-something undergraduate. I'd been introduced to this and other works of critical urban theory—especially to Castells's *Urban Question* and Harvey's *Social Justice and the City*—by Trevor Jones, a gifted, maverick Social Studies teacher at what was then Liverpool Polytechnic. I didn't quite know it at the time but Jones's lectures would change the course of life, such that I can still talk about them 30 years on. Under Jones's tutelage, I'd already decided that I was a Marxist and Pahl a liberal; so *Whose City?* was a vital text only insofar as it took me beyond Chicago School urban ecology, propelling me onwards to the hard-core critical material I yearned for. Jones put urban managerialism pithily in context: Imagine the city is a large cake; imagine you cut the cake into a series of slices, with each slice representing some scarce resource; a thick, creamy slice here, a slither over there. Managerialism tells us how that cake gets divided up and who gets such and such a slice and why; but it doesn't tell us who bakes the cake, nor does it say why those urban resources are "scarce" in the first place. "Who decides?" is one thing; but "Who decides who decides?" is another question again. And there Marxism comes into its own.

In those days, I remember carrying *Whose City?* around with me in my black denim jacket pocket; a small-cut Penguin paperback, it fitted perfectly. In retrospect, I think the books that made a lasting

6. Pahl, *Whose City?*, p. 275.

impression on me all somehow fitted into one of my pockets; they were transportable, moving theory, particularly as I navigated around the new cities I'd soon find myself in. These books were theoretical street guides to the hidden structures of the city, atlases to vital parts of the city that weren't always visible to any naked eye. This would be an invaluable lesson university curriculum would only partly help convey. (Manuel Castells's bulky *Urban Question*, of course, didn't fit into any coat pocket; I suspect I was happy to transport it under my arm, hoping people might actually believe I understood its contents!)

Quite recently, I took that Pahl book, that same tatty edition, to a conference in Hong Kong commemorating Pahl's life and death, justly entitled "Whose City?".[7] In my contribution I reflected upon what Pahl's book was and might still be today, might still offer concerned urbanists who know better than ever to whom cities like Hong Kong really belong. One thing I noticed this time, which I hadn't noticed back then, was that my copy of *Whose City?* had been withdrawn from Bradford College Library in 1984, during the fear and loathing of Thatcher's first term. When I mentioned this in my talk the audience began to laugh. We all began to laugh because we all knew—or most of us knew—that the Thatcherite project was at that moment in full flight actively dismantling Pahl's theoretical object and political subject. His commitment to welfare statism was under fire from all quarters; multiple levels of local and national government would feel Thatcher's "free market" heat, abolished and abused and recalibrated to suit the whims of an ascendant private sector.

Back then this posed some pretty tough intellectual and political questions for my friends and I who, in those heady days, were more fuck-you anarchists than clever, tactical and theoretically-informed Marxists. We passed a lot of our time wondering how to fill the

7. The conference, organized by Ray Forrest and Bart Wissink, took place at the Department of Public Policy, City University of Hong Kong on May 24–25, 2013. Pahl himself died of cancer in June 2011, aged 75. In a *Guardian* obituary (July 26, 2011), Claire Wallace highlights Pahl's "restless intelligence, his sharp mind and equally sharp tongue. Ray never courted easily popularity. He chose what he saw as the right way, which was often the hard way. You may not have liked what he said, but he never hid his views."

post-punk void, and hated the bourgeois state with serious venom. We wanted to smash it, get rid of its oppressive sway. So when Thatcher started to do just that, we were left wondering where to turn. Did we want that nanny state back? Life had been boring and programmed with it, but maybe things were going to be much worse without it? In retrospect, 1984 seems a bit of a watershed, the significant year of contamination: Ronald Reagan had begun his second term and the Iron Lady had survived the Brighton Bombing; the IRA's attempt to finish Thatcher off had the perverse effect of only setting her more solidly on her way, propelling her full-kilter into dismantling the post-war social contract between capital and labor, taking on (and taking out) organized labor and organized opposition in the process; Arthur Scargill and the miners, as well as Militant in Liverpool, took it full on the chin.

Thatcherism frontal assault on welfare provision, her blatant class warfare, actually created a generation of lazy entrepreneurs in Britain, capitalists who had no need to innovate because business was handed to them on a Tory silver platter. And those remaining urban managers no longer concerned themselves with allocative redistributive justice; most wouldn't even know what the phrase meant. Instead, their working day began to be passed applying cost-benefit analysis to calculate efficiency models, devising new business paradigms for delivering social services at minimum cost; services got contracted-out to low-ball bidders, and whole government departments were dissolved or replaced by new units of non-accountable "post-political" middle-managers, whose machinations are about as publicly transparent as mud.

A dramatic transformation of urban governance was wrought, a shift from managerialism to entrepreneurialism, from social investment in the urban realm to the speculative binge of the urban itself; use-values had uses only because they were exchange-values; cities' "scarce" resources quickly became speculative stock, new futures and options for expanded capital accumulation by dispossession. Yet while we know that this shift from managerialism to entrepreneurialism involved disjuncture and rupture, that it reveled in forcible implementation, we also know with hindsight how it involved a certain morphing and role switching of protagonists, with revolving doors between public managers and private entrepreneurs, between managerial entrepreneurs and entrepreneurial managers. (In lots of ways this toing and froing across ideological boundaries made its debut in the 1980s in France, during Mitterrand's presidency, when radical ex-'68ers became diehard neoliberal politicians and media pundits. For good reason Guy Debord always said that the society of "integrated spectacle" was pioneered in France.)

And if, in Britain, the initial thrust had been Thatcher's, then John Major and notably Tony Blair expertly finished the job. In that sense, corporate, financial and state power are now stitched together with barely any trace of a seam. Politicians and civil servants, bankers and CEOs, job-share and job-swap; public faces and private concerns are shamelessly interchangeable and mutually beneficial for both careers and bank accounts. As Seumas Milne has pointed out, the doors between the public and the private "are no longer just revolving but spinning, and people charged with protecting public interests are bought and sold with barely a fig leaf of regulation."[8] "Take David Hartnett," says Milne, "head of tax at HM Revenue & Customs until last year and the man whose 'sweetheart deals' allowed Starbucks and Vodafone to avoid paying billions in tax. He now works for the giant City accountancy firm Deloitte, which works for Vodafone." "The cabinet secretary, Jeremy Heywood, is the living embodiment of the revolving door, having moved effortlessly from the Treasury to Blair's office to the investment bank Morgan Stanley and back to work for David Cameron."

Along the way, the public coffers have been raided, plundered by hybrid public–private bodies like PFIs (Private Finance Initiatives), the brainchild of John Major, which have helped themselves to urban infrastructure—ports, roads, schools, railways, electricity grids, and God knows what else, not only in Britain but throughout the world. When the going is good, PFIs—government-sponsored private companies with zero public accountability—amass considerable booty; when things go belly-up, the government steps in to bail them out because the continuation of the particular utility serves

8. Seumas Milne, "Corporate Power has turned Britain into a Corrupt State," *Guardian*, June 5, 2013.

a vital public necessity and can't go under. It's an all-win situation for everybody, apart from the ordinary tax payer and consumer. As such, the neoliberal stakes have profoundly ratcheted up since Thatcher's day: what we've witnessed isn't so much a privatization as a *financialization* of public infrastructure and services, speculative quackery enabling windfall gains (when equity is cashed in) for a tiny minority of bosses and shareholders, some of whom are supposedly public servants.

* * *

So, returning to the question *Whose City?*, the answer, perhaps, is pretty clear: it's the parasites' city, and their progeny is a species we can now label the *parasitic city*. A parasite, remember, is an organism that feeds off a larger "host" organism, an uninvited diner at the lodge who doesn't pay for their grub. Parasites chomp away at the common-wealth the world over, eating away inside the social body, stripping peoples's assets, foreclosing homes, *dispossessing* value rather than contributing anything toward its creation. In parasitic cities, social wealth is consumed through conspicuously wasteful enterprises, administered by parasitic elites, our very own aristocracy (the 1 percent) who squander generative capacity by thriving exclusively from unproductive activities: they roll dice on the stock market, profit from unequal exchanges, guzzle at the public trough; they filch rents and treat land as a pure financial and speculative asset, as a form of fictitious capital.

The only thing parasites need to do is sit on property, mobilize monopoly power, and charge somebody else a premium for using or entering it. "One part of society," Marx says in Volume Three of *Capital* (Chapter 46), "thus exacts tribute from another for the permission to inhabit the earth, as landed property in general assigns the landlord the privilege of exploiting the terrestrial body, the bowels of the earth, the air, and thereby the maintenance and development of life." "It is the ground-rent," Marx was wont to emphasize, "and not the house, which forms the actual object of building speculation in rapidly growing cities, especially where construction is carried on as an industry." Artificially created scarcity jacks up land values; financial and property interests promote redevelopment on the land toward "higher" and "better" capitalistic uses, toward future increased exchange-values pocketed as class-monopoly rents. Parasites hatch land and infrastructural grabs and get their friends in government to issue "eminent domain" edicts, legalizing their parasitic predilections. Parasites thrive in both the private and public sectors and especially flourish where those sectors merge as one. Parasites do everything they can to leech blood money, flattening themselves off the backs of social labor. And these days they brandish any pretext to do so under the ruse of a politics of austerity.

In the 1950s, the development economist Bert Hoselitz first coined the notion of "parasitic" cities. In *Sociological Aspects of Economic Growth* [1960], Hoselitz wondered whether cities in the developing world, with their "backward" economies, would turn out to be parasitical or generative.[9] ("World Cities" theorist John Friedmann would later pick up on this for thinking about Latin American urbanization.) Generative cities, said Hoselitz, have a favorable impact on economic growth; parasitic cities produce the opposite, negative effect, syphoning off economic resources for the enrichment of privileged urban classes who render no real productive services in return. Generative cities reallocate the bulk of its surplus and accumulated wealth, giving it back in the form of investment that benefits production and people, public infrastructure and human capital. Parasitic cities, conversely, have their wealth squandered by a non-working yet all-consuming elite; a parasitic form of urbanization, reflective of the parasitic nature of this urbanized elite, thereby ensues.

It's ironic to think that under Hoselitz's (and Friedmann's) thesis, parasitic usually meant "developing" cities; generative cities were *our* cities, in the "developed" world, whose industrial heartlands like Pittsburgh and Detroit, to say nothing of New York and London, once made things, provided real jobs and generated wealth. Now, though, in these latter places, cappuccino-sipping elites idly sit around in chic bars and cafés, checking stocks and shares on their Blackberries or

9. Bert Hoselitz, *The Sociological Aspects of Economic Growth*, Free Press, Chicago, 1960.

iPhones, while the designer clothes they sport are manufactured in brutal garment factories in "generative cities" like Dhaka and Jakarta. Still, the reality of the situation is that parasitic urban elites consume the social wealth *everywhere*, in the developing as well as developed world. In fact, the binary between developed and developing worlds no longer seems analytically or politically tenable, given parasitic urbanism nestles everywhere and marks the pathological condition of our neoliberal urban age. The parasitic city, in short, is a cancerous cell in the molecular structure of our global urban fabric.

In the urban studies literature we hear a lot of hype about "global cities" as engines of economic growth, as "growth machines." Yet one really has to wonder if this is true, if global cities nowadays are about the "wealth of nations" (as Jane Jacobs put it in the 1980s). One doesn't have to look too hard or too deeply to see how most of the world's biggest metropolises have economies established on activities justifiably categorized as parasitic. World cities are giant arenas where the most rabid activity is the activity of rabidly extorting land rent, of making land pay anyway it can; of dispatching all non-parasitic activities to some other part of town (as Engels recognized long ago), so as to help this rental maximization. Generative activities frequently mean dirt and grime, and usually involve dirty and grimy people, which is very bad for parasitic business. (Parasites flourish amid cleanliness, where immunity has been broken down.)

Parasites have colonized some of the swankiest parts of urban areas. Take London. Private equity firms don't just skew stock markets, they also commit grand larceny in property markets. Mayfair is notoriously home to hedge fund firms, discreet behind their iron-railed Victorian mews, spotlessly painted white. As Nicholas Shaxson says, "Mayfair would be far more economically productive if it were turned into a giant waste-disposal centre."[10] That London is becoming rich pickings for the world's super-elite is well documented.[11] Its property market is the new, safer investment haven, a stock-market in exile, a giant

10. Nicholas Shaxson, "The Zombies of Mayfair," *New Statesman*, June 28, 2013, pp. 31–5.
11. Cf. Michael Goldfarb, "London's Great Exodus," *New York Times*, October 12, 2013, p. SR5.

global reserve currency with bonanza rates of annualized return, generating an inflationary spiral that squeezes other, more modest sectors of the housing and rental market, putting intense pressure on lower- and middle-income people. In 2011, at the height of the eurozone crisis, Goldfarb reports how the obscenely wealthy of two countries at the epicenter of cataclysm—Greece and Italy—fearing single currency collapse, got their cash out of euros and converted it into London's sterling property market, buying £400 millions' worth of its bricks and mortar. Hot money from China, Singapore, and India, too, Goldfarb says, has flowed in at torrential rates, meaning "an astonishing £83 billion worth of London properties were purchased in 2012 with no financing—all cash purchases." And Cameron's Britain is auspicious, given its gentle property tax regime and lax regulatory environment for the rich. New York Mayor Mike Bloomberg, for instance, pays £2,143.30 per annum on his £20 million Kensington home.

Spearheading parasitic urban predilections—legitimizing them as a cultural force—are, meanwhile, assorted "creative classes." American urbanist Richard Florida has made a lucrative career promoting urban boho-chic, yet in many (if not most) cases, "creation" here seems more akin to inventing new niches for further rounds of dispossession and contagious parasitic proliferation: creative accountancy and creative ways to avoid paying tax; creative devices to gouge fees from ordinary citizens (especially in utility bills); creative finagling of stock markets; creative new patents and apps that tap hitherto untapped markets; creative destruction of competition to garner inflated monopoly rents and profits; creative excuses to cadge money from the state. The list goes on, creatively. And when they parachute into cities, these creative and cognitive classes have little use of public infrastructure anyway; their lives are so utterly privatized, geared only toward individual, market-oriented goods, that they bid-up land values and property prices and hasten the abandonment of the public realm in the creative bargain.

* * *

The question, *Whose City?*, accordingly, might not be the most interesting one to ask today. The more pressing concern is what can we do about parasites? How can "we" develop a vaccine to eradicate the parasites within our social body? How to reclaim the parasitic city for people, for the "host" community? Are there any prophylactics to prevent the further proliferation of parasites? How to develop civic immunity? One initial, reformist measure is to stop the billions of pounds and dollars draining from the public finances because of corporate tax avoidance. Governments insist on belt-tightening austerity policies, running down collective consumption provision and screwing the ordinary tax payer at the same time as they turn a blind eye on tax dodging companies, carving themselves up and re-registering their head offices in tax havens like the Cayman Islands, Monaco or Luxembourg; or else entrusting ownership on phony overseas partners or close relatives who've never ever set foot on the said companies' premises. Already, in this regard, a groundswell of opposition has developed. Grassroots organizations like UK Uncut have adopted rambunctious and brilliantly innovative direct action "occupations," creating scandals around tax-avoiding parasites like the swanky London department store Fortnum & Mason and Vodafone (who had a handy 0 percent income tax rate for 2012). UK Uncut have likewise launched concerted campaigns against HSBC, Royal Bank of Scotland and Barclays and other Dodge City banks and financial institutions.[12]

Maybe the greatest reform and strongest prophylactic against parasitic invasion is *democracy*, a strengthening of participatory democracy in the face of too much representative democracy, especially when representation is made by public servants intent on defending private gain. Government as we currently know must be terminated. We need to root out the virus, all those blood suckers who leech life from the generative social body. The notion that "we" represent the "99%" is a fruitful beginning at identifying the minority parasite that contaminates the majority culture. Some

12. For a spirited account of tax crimes and misdemeanors, see Richard Brooks's *The Great Tax Robbery: How Britain Became a Tax Haven for Fat Cats and Big Business* (Oneworld Publications, London, 2013).

planned shrinkage of the financial sector seems in order, waging war on monetary blood sucking in the same vein as the ruling class waged war on public services in the 1970s and 1980s. And here, too, that preeminent parasitic organism, the leech of landed property—"the monstrous power wielded by landed property," Marx called it, "expelling people from the earth as a dwelling-place"—needs to be expunged, democratized by some Community Land Trust that can reinvigorate a fresh notion of the public realm, one not owned and managed by any centralized state but owned and run by a collectivization of people, federated, communal and truly responsive to citizens' needs.

In an odd sort of way, Ray Pahl's urban managerialist thesis still instructs, still says something meaningful about twenty-first-century parasitic urbanism. Indeed, the whole question of "managers," of those middle-management "social gatekeepers" Pahl impugned so many years ago, remains analytically vital for pinpointing administrative culpability; or, if you will, is still politically vital for breaking the "weakest link" in a concatenation of parasitic cells. To that degree, struggling for democracy means loosening the diktat that these anonymous, unaccountable, behind-closed-doors middle-managers, various euro functionaries and international technocrats have over our culture. Breaking the weakest link implies waging war not only against the massively complex and alienating divisions of labor we have today, but also against the even more massively alienating bureaucratic compartmentalizations that rule over us (in both the public and private sectors), those precisely orchestrated by Pahlian entrepreneurial managers who mediate between us and the 1 percent, and who stabilize and calibrate the imbalance globally.

The problematic is as much Kafkaseque as Marxist or Weberian, as struggling against the parasite within. To do so we need to redouble mass civil disobedience, continually affirm our democratic desires. That way a different meme might get created and collectively exchanged, counteracting parasitic invasion. A meme is a cultural transmitter, a messenger particle carrying an idea, a symbol or a buzz concept that catches on, that's communicable between people, that solidifies group identity. ("Meme" is shorthand for the Greek *mimeme*, meaning something imitative.) "When you plant a fertile meme in my mind," says biologist Richard Dawkins in *The Selfish Gene*, "you literally parasitize my brain, turning it into a vehicle for the meme's propagation in just the way a virus may parasitize the genetic mechanism of the host cell."[13] In this light we might say that neoliberalism is a meme that has parasitized our brains as well as our society over the past 20 years or more, and has entered our culture in a way that looks like a highly speeded up genetic revolution, but has really nothing to do with a genetic revolution. There's nothing "natural" going on here: parasitic agents and commissars, institutions and lobbyists have cajoled and bullied and seduced us into accepting this meme as a given, ensuring that the idea has evolved memically, imitatively, to the selfish advantage of the 1 percent.

An appeal for a permanent "meme war," for revolters to battle under the banner of a new meme, is, then, to propagate a different political-economic paradigm, one antagonistic to the existing order, transforming and even erasing the institutions that spread this old meme.[14] The task remains: How to incubate such an alternative meme, how to dose up on it to strengthen our immunity system? How might it circulate as a prophylactic within the generative cells of our urban politic, permanently ridding us of parasites. To frame it that way is to paraphrase Ray Pahl: it is to say that middle-managers

13. Richard Dawkins, *The Selfish Gene*, Oxford University Press, Oxford, 1989, p. 192.
14. The call for a "meme war" has been most creatively articulated by Adbusters editor Kalle Lasn in his collection *Meme Wars: The Creative Destruction of Neoclassical Economics* (Penguin Books, London, 2012), sporting a sub-sub-title of "A Real World Economics Textbook." *Meme Wars*, dedicated to Guy Debord (amongst others), is a 400-page reincarnation of Situationist agitprop, full of wonderfully inventive graphics, peppered with slogans and polemical essays that voice the visceral gut feeling that society as we currently know it sucks, that it sucks blood. What we might be witnessing here is what Debord himself called "domination's falling rate of profit": as neoliberalism spreads to the scale of the whole of social space it consequently devours its own comparative advantage and somehow "plots against itself" (cf. Guy Debord, *Comments on the Society of the Spectacle*, p. 84).

remain bearers of the parasitic meme; they remain, therefore, as central as ever to the new urban problematic, to a new democratic problematic in which politicians and their administrators (or is that the other way around?) no longer even pretend to want to change anything significant.

Afterword: The Parasitic Mode of Urbanization

Finance capital doesn't want liberty, it wants domination.

—Rudolf Hilferding

In the early 1970s, when major-scale crises propelled advanced nations' economies into giddy nosedives, a critical school of political-economic thought, Regulation Theory, made a pretty convincing case for *periodizing* twentieth-century capitalism. What we were seeing back then, Regulationist theorists said, was a critical rupturing of one "regime of accumulation" and its superimposition by another. Accumulation prevailed, needless to say, still reigned as a systemic impulse, as the inner logic of capitalism, roughly along the lines that Marx sketched out in Volume One of *Capital*; but how this capitalist system went about its accumulation business was in a state of crisis-induced flux, was necessarily transmogrifying into a qualitatively different form, into something that would soon bear the label "post-Fordist."[1]

1. See Michel Aglietta, *A Theory of Capitalist Regulation* (Verso, London, 1974); Robert Boyer, *The Regulation School: A Critical Introduction* (Columbia University Press, New York, 1990). Regulation School rejects all rational "economic purity," like perfect markets and perfect competition, etc., etc., the usual propaganda that gets inculcated in business schools and on Ivy League 101 Econ courses. From a Regulationist standpoint, economic relations are "embedded" (as Karl Polyani might have said) in a social fabric and can't exist without this social fabric; they can't somehow be "disembedded." As such, what bourgeois economists deem irksome "externalities" are really only features "internal" (i.e. endogenous and essential) to the normal functioning and, more especially, normal malfunctioning of market economies.

Regulation Theory's other insight was that every regime of accumulation requires a corresponding "mode of regulation," its very own set of political institutions and social mechanisms, its own supporting agents and assuaging ideologies, all of which somehow keep things in working order, keep a regime of accumulation's wheels of motion lubricated with the owner's recommended engine oil, calibrated by the right tools to precise degrees of specification. Hence the other vital element of Regulation Theory: the notion of *reproduction*, how the reproduction of capital seemingly takes place even under systematic breakdown. Thus, for Regulationists, there's a crucial reciprocity between the regime of accumulation and its mode of regulation, between a historically specific capitalist economy and its civil society; each needs one another just as base and superstructure, social relations and productive forces coexist for any classically-minded Marxist. Upheavals on one flank give rise to upheavals on the other flank; the two flanks condition one another in dynamic and dialectical complementarity.

Regulation Theory offers a brilliant take on cyclical as well as structural crises, on fluctuations in economic growth and on the political sociology that (de)regulates these fluctuations. Yet while Regulationists have never directly discussed the urban question, it's perhaps not too hard to project their analytical devices onto the plane of urbanization itself, to frame our current global urban condition as a regime of accumulation and mode of (de)regulation that could be best described as *parasitic*; a shift even from a form of urban governance once labeled "entrepreneurial" to another, significantly different urban process and concomitant urban question.

The latest global crisis erupted in August 2007, in the United States, with its subprime mortgage fiasco. This crisis soon hit Europe, and struck at the very (weak) heart of the world's financial system in early October 2008. Yet perhaps the roots of this crisis, as well as the inauguration of the parasitic urban form, lie in the East Asian crisis of 1997–98, which, as Michel Aglietta has said, "marked the world economy's entry into a new, inherently unstable, accumulation regime."[2] He may be right: the global turbulence resultant of 1997–98

2. Michel Aglietta, "The European Vortex," *New Left Review*, No. 75, May–June 2012, p. 15.

heralded the real subsumption of the economy under the drive for shareholder value; and prominent therein has been the quest for easy, short-term returns, of which rental income forms a vital component (in London, annualized rates of return on rents now top 10 percent).

The new urban question for radical theory thus means figuring out the curiously novel mode of urbanization we have in our midst today, the phoenix arising out of the burnout ashes of 1970s' crises, that bullishly entered the Thatcherite and Reaganite 1980s, that consolidated itself in the late 1990s and early 2000s (especially after 9/11), and that now, post-2008, has no scruples about raiding urban coffers everywhere and mobilizing "scarce" urban resources as speculative investment stock, as new futures and options for expanded capital accumulation by dispossession in times of capitalist crises, as new rounds of primitive accumulation in times of public sector austerity.

The new urban question for radical politics, for progressive people everywhere, thus means figuring out what to do about all this? One response to this regime of accumulation and mode of urbanization, its political contraflow, might be: is it possible to similarly periodize a mode of dissent, a revolt against the dominant order? Maybe it's possible to identify and nurture a new brand of progressive dissenters, people who symbolize and enact a different, historically specific disposition to make trouble, to protest, to revolt against the structures of neoliberal parasitic power? In this afterword, let me try to list several new (or at least newish) categories of oppositional forces we might want to consider as well as bolster:

1. *Secret Agents* are people who devote their very lives and being to the radical cause. They may be professional organizers and tacticians, plotting and dissenting, often clandestinely, writing and printing militant literature, existing to spread the word and fight the power. Though secret agents have existed from radical time immemorial, nowadays they may be black bloc'er anarchists, Marxists, socialists, autonomous and Anonymous communists of assorted stripes and persuasions, both young and veteran alike, who, with Occupy, with the Arab Spring, with revolts in the *banlieues*, with the *Indignados* and Greeks, with stuff going on

in Turkey, have now found focus, some medium through which they can channel and refract their energies and dissatisfactions. Their militancy is at once open and concealed, known to some yet hidden from others. The label "secret agent" appeals because it conjures up some shady radical presence, a presence through a certain societal absence, a menacing figure who haunts, like the Verloc character about which Joseph Conrad ironized in his 1906 eponymous novel. Indeed, Verloc, the said Secret Agent, planned to dynamite the Greenwich Meridian much as Occupiers would love to see the whole Wall Street scene blow, Verloc who intended to assault the organization of capitalist time much as occupiers seek to assault the whole organization of capitalist finance. Of course, Conrad created a grotesque character with Verloc, a social and sexual deviant, partly because of his foreignness (he was half-French!), partly because he didn't fit the standard norms of respectability. Whatever his domestic failings and selfish conceitedness, Conrad said Verloc's mind "lacked profundity,"[3] that Verloc's failing was a failing of feeling, a failing of feeling the complexity of the situation, a failing of feeling real compassion for the dispossessed; we might say that as a secret agent Verloc was a stereotype not an archetype.

These days, secret agents conspire with a great deal more sophistication and complexity, with a great deal more feeling and compassion; at least they should. Maybe *The Man Who Was Thursday*, G.K. Chesterton's whimsical retelling of the revolutionary mind, published a year after Conrad's, is more informative and sustainable. It's a suitably dialectical tale of raffish Lucian Gregory, the "walking blasphemy, a blend of angel and sage" (who turns out to be the mysterious anarchist President, "Sunday"), and poet-cop Gabriel Syme, whose "rebellion against rebellion" eventually led him to rebel against his rebellion against rebellion;[4]

3. Joseph Conrad, *The Secret Agent: A Simple Tale*, Penguin Classics, London, 2007, p. 185.
4. G.K. Chesterton, *The Man Who Was Thursday: A Nightmare*, Penguin Red Classics, London, 2007. No stranger to this line of thinking, Guy Debord wrote, in *Comments on the Society of the Spectacle* (p. 11), that "the highest

2. If Secret Agents have a "cover," *Double Agents* conceal their dual identities from the broader public. Their being isn't "either/or" but "both/and." In practice, this makes for a strange, schizoid practice, a deeper political idealism lurking behind a socially conventional pragmatism, a person in society who is rebelling against society. The stuff of the 99% doubtless consists of many double agents: they earn a living to equip themselves to overthrow what earning a living really means. Marx affirmed double agents; his well-heeled friend and benefactor Friedrich Engels, after all, was one, managing the textile mill his communist ideals wanted to tear apart. Marx recognized how the developmental impulse of modern capitalism dowsed claims to holy purity in the damp waters of market profanity; everybody needs to find work to live, and that finding work inevitably means producing capital for somebody else. Marx knew that the resourcefulness of the bourgeoisie always means there's a market for radical ideas, that modern capitalism creates specific market niches, plunders these ideas, commodifies them, charges a fee to read them, exploits the brains that created these ideas, re-appropriating them in order to generate more profit and accumulate capital. But Marx at the same time knew how markets also help disseminate radical ideas, help them find broader audiences, while providing (limited) income for the double agents who have these radical ideas, and who work at trying to bite the hand that feeds them. Trade unions should (though usually don't) conspire to incubate double agents, a rank-and-file membership concerned with immediate pay and conditions yet that also has its horizons open, that works to live beyond work, that labors to transform the labor relations underpinning work, knowing in the meanwhile that workers and their families need to live. Any radical artist, too, who wants their revolutionary art and wares to find broader publics knows about the hazards and possibilities of double agency. They sometimes follow what Walter Benjamin said of poet Charles Baudelaire: that he was the "double agent of his class," "an agent of secret

---

ambition of the integrated spectacle is still to turn secret agents into revolutionaries and revolutionaries into secret agents."

discontent of his class within its rule,"[5] a species who is the very product of modern life, with its complex role playing and ambivalences, its tangled loyalties and multiple identities. Double agents revel in the tormented freedoms and contradictions these ambivalences engender, for living as well as for creating, and sometimes thrive off the double binds and double liberties within a singular body politic;

3. *Maggots in the apple* is the evocative phrase Henri Lefebvre took from French novelist Stendhal. In the first few decades of the nineteenth century, Stendhal described a "new romanticism" in the air, a brazenly utopian response to the problems of an emergent technological and industrial civilization, problems that remain ours today. In the early 1960s, when Lefebvre wrote *Introduction to Modernity*, he spotted a renewal of both classical and modern romanticism fighting back against the crushing irrational rationality of a bourgeois modernity run amok, updating the project Stendhal announced in the 1820s: "At last," Stendhal wrote in *Racine and Shakespeare* (1823), "the great day will come when the youth will awaken; this noble youth will be amazed to realize how long and how seriously it has been applauding such colossal inanities."[6] "It requires courage to be a romantic," Stendhal said, "because one must take a risk." Lefebvre concluded *Introduction to Modernity* by saying there was a "new attitude" drifting in the breeze: revolts, acts of insubordination, protests, abstentions, rebellions were there and felt; Stendhal was a man of the late twentieth century. Stendhal's romanticism affirmed disparate elements of society: "women, young people, political rebels, exiles, intellectuals, half-crazed debauchees, drunks, misfits, successive and abortive geniuses, *arrivistes*, Parisian dandies and provincial snobs." Perhaps their historical counterparts today are the downsized "post-work" victims of a right-sizing capitalist corporate ethic, which "sets workers free" as business cycles dip

5. Walter Benjamin, *Selected Writing: Volume 2, 1927–1934*, Harvard University Press, Cambridge, MA, 2003, p. 92, n. 300.
6. Stendhal, *Racine and Shakespeare*, in Henri Lefebvre, *Introduction to Modernity*, Verso, London, 1995, p. 239.

and as austerity measures grip; and the maggots now constitute a huge mass of sub-, under- and unemployed workers, a relative surplus population, working, if they ever find work, insecurely, in McJobs, on temporary contracts, on workfare programs and in internships, students and post-students who know that before them lies a dark, deep abyss that's about to engulf them, a black hole of the labor market and debt. This ragged array of people now attempts to live out within everyday bourgeois society their ideal solutions to bourgeois society, challenging its "moral" economic order, surviving in its core, "like a maggot in an apple," trying to eat their way out from the inside. Stendhal is a man of the twenty-first-century;

4. *Great Escapers* take to *flight* as a form of fight and express a spirit of critical positivity. They have absolutely no truck with existing society and go it alone, alone with others, to create alternative radical communities and communes, frequently self-sufficient, both in the city and the countryside, self-valorizing the urbanization of both. Their modus operandi is precisely the opposite of Kafka's K.: instead of trying to enter the inner recesses of the castle, of the citadel of contemporary capitalism, instead of trying to find doors to knock on and people to complain to, demanding their "rights," real great escapers burrow out under the castle's ramparts and ask for nothing. They dig tunnels and construct exit trails; they organize, with great caution, invisible escape committees; and they hope their tunnels will be long enough and sufficiently deep enough to reach freedom, ubiquitous enough to converge with other tunnels. And if enough people dig, the whole surface superstructure might one day give away entirely, after everybody has left. What remains will implode in one great big heap of rubble—like the Berlin Wall. The Great Escape suggests something subterranean, something organized and tactical, something practical and concrete. It begins below, at ground level, and doesn't float up in the air, abstractly, plonking itself down undemocratically. A lot of liberals and radicals still believe that the central object of any struggle isn't to orchestrate escape tunnels but to destroy the social structures and institutions that underwrite human captivity, that support privilege and

authority, that define the castle on the hill. They say that one needs to abolish the conditions of mass subordination, destroy the logic of prison camps as well as the processes that give rise to camp mentality. One needs to negate the contradiction between inmate and warder, they say, before one can begin to create a passage to freedom. But demolishing the neoliberal structural order is arguably a project destined to suffer the same trials and frustrations K. suffered when he tried to break into his castle, when he tried to find a well-grounded confidence for further and greater struggles that should have followed yet which always eluded him.

Here we might want to remember Walter Benjamin's brilliant essay on Kafka, at the tenth-anniversary of the latter's death (in 1934).[7] In it, Benjamin introduces Potemkin, Catherine the Great's depressive, drunken chancellor, who, in one unusually long low, retreats to his room, barring everybody entry. But nothing can be done without Potemkin's signature. So official business piles up; policies can't be enacted and grave irregularities result; Russian ministries come to a standstill. Catherine and top civil servants are at their wits' end. Then, one day, a young, headstrong minor clerk called Schuwalkin enters, wondering what's up. Schuwalkin isn't impressed with the inactivity. So he grabs the papers and sets off through galleries, along the corridors, to Potemkin's gloomy bedchamber. In he marches, without knocking, without even saying a word, foisting the documents under the nose of the bedridden chancellor. Dipping his plume in ink, he hands it to the startled Potemkin. Absent-mindedly, sleepily, the latter executes the first signature, then a second, then a third, and eventually all. Schuwalkin returns to the ministers who bend over the documents with dismay. Document after document is signed "Schuwalkin, Schuwalkin, Schuwalkin . . ." The tale, says Benjamin, strikes like a messenger. The zealous Schuwalkin, like Kafka's K., has a brush with authority, is partly assuaged, yet ultimately comes away frustrated. Those authorities, mysterious

7. "Franz Kafka: On the Tenth Anniversary of his Death," in Walter Benjamin, *One-Way Street and Other Writings*, Penguin Books, London, 2009.

and secluded in their dark attics within attics, along corridors off corridors, are there, sometimes glimpsed, sometimes even challenged, yet always—or seemingly always—elude us. Schuwalkin's story is our story, almost one hundred years after Kafka's death. Benjamin propels Kafka and his world into our world. It's a world in which we progressives either come on like the youthful, confident Schuwalkin, swashbuckling our way in, in head-on confrontation, yet achieve little—apart from often getting hurt; or else we stand idle like those feckless politicians around Potemkin, inactive and idealess, waiting desperately for better times ahead. Contemporary great escapers need to be savvier than Schuwalkin, in both their activity and inactivity, learning how to wait (as Guy Debord said) and how to move;

5. *Great Refusers* take to *fight* as a form of flight and express a spirit of negative defiance, immortalized by Herbert Marcuse's *One Dimensional Man* [1964], his no-holds-barred outcry "against that which is."[8] In refusing to play the game, in voicing NO, in individually and collectively downing tools, great refusers already begin to create another dimension to life, give renewed breadth and depth to it, re-sublimate what has been de-sublimated, denied by a delusional "happy consciousness." Better to sport an unhappy, dissatisfied mien, Marcuse thought, with a frustrated libido that still functions, that still flows with the energy of the Life Instinct, than have your vital center bought off, sensually deprived by the instant gratification of society's techo-gismos. In 1964, Marcuse said a "Total Administration" permeated all reality, possessed the body and souls of everyday people; it didn't. Though it almost did during the 1980s; perhaps now, circa 2014, stronger claims can be made for its supposed near omnipotence, for its inbuilt calibration in defense laboratories and executive offices, in governments and middle-managers, in timekeepers and machines, in efficiency experts and mass communications, in publicity agencies and multinational corporations, in supranational organizations and universities—in all those institutions and organizations that

8. Herbert Marcuse, *One Dimensional Man: The Ideology of Industrial Society*, Sphere Books, London, 1968, p. 63 (emphasis added).

somehow power and profit from the process of urbanization. (Think of how many universities are the biggest land grabbers and arch-gentrifiers.) The Total Administration's consenting means liquidates opposition, absorbs opposition, or else tries to; the Reality Principle vanquishes over the Pleasure Principle, convincing people that Reality is the *only* principle. Still, there are others who "prefer not to," who desist from wanting in, both quietly (like the passive negation of Melville's scrivener, Bartleby) and noisily; and they're now not only a substratum of society's outcasts and outsiders, of Beats and hipsters, as Marcuse insisted, but ordinary folk as well, a growing majority who find themselves outside the "democratic" process, redundant and disenfranchised in a system of increasing technological rationality and economic inequality. The "I prefer not to" cannot be suppressed, the "non-coincidence" between the self we are and self that society wants us to be. It's a non-coincidence, Sartre said in *Existentialism is a Humanism*, between an individual subject and his or her social being, a gap that bequeaths dissent, has to breed dissent.

* * *

Doubtless dissenters here can fall into more than one of these categories, and might even fall *between* categories. Their respective constitution and organizing causes, be they romantically idealist or pragmatically realist, can likewise change over time, can shift and morph subject to personal and political circumstances. Indeed, the changing nature of their revolt suggests that this falling in and out of categories, and between categories, will make dissent both positively and negatively charged, a constant toing and froing that makes revolt more flexible and adaptive. Meanwhile, all categories need each other, will reinforce one another, offer both offensive fronts and rearguard defenses. And the efficacy of any dissent will likely be predicated on how these dissenters organize themselves internally yet coordinate themselves externally, reach out to one another, create a bigger kaleidoscope, a more inclusive constellation of dissent that coexists horizontally and democratically, both overground and underground.

Such a constellation can shine different light on things, create a new cosmological political aura.

In its cosmic radiance and human heterogeneity, this democratic constellation would represent what Rousseau labeled "the general will," a will, we know, that's infallible when it congeals democratically. The people can't be wrong, Rousseau always insisted, but they can, he warned, often be deceived, deceived into acting for what isn't in their own interests. One of the most effective forms of deceiving people is *fear*, and today a big perpetrator of fear is *austerity*, the language our ruling class bawls in our ears and booms out over the airwaves—that as it goes on its own spending spree. Austerity creates fear because people fear for their jobs, fear for their livelihoods, fear they can't pay their mortgages, won't have anywhere to live. People fear the future. Austerity, in this sense, is a European 9/11: you mightn't like what we're doing, governments say, but hey, believe us, the alternative is much worse. In fact there is no alternative. And, as with 9/11, anything antagonistic to this program, including people who contest it, are deemed unpatriotic, even terroristic. Austerity is ruling-class ideology, manufactured consent, music to the ears of European Central Bankers and *comprador* bourgeoisies of various European countries. They're *comprador* bourgeoisie because they're puppets of these central bankers, including bankers and financiers in the U.S.[9]

As well as serving handy ideological purposes, austerity also fits neatly with the material needs of those in power, and those who can economically prosper from that power. Austerity enables parasitic predilections to flourish by opening up hitherto closed market niches; it lets accumulation by dispossession continue apace, condoning the flogging off of public sector assets, its selling them off at fire sale prices, the free giveaways, the privatizations, all done in the name of cost control, of trimming bloated public budgets. What were once

9. In a review of a recent batch of books on the Eurozone crisis, Susan Watkins points to Britain's historic "Trojan Horse" role for U.S. interests in Europe (the phrase is De Gaulle's). "David Cameron," she writes, "has lately spared no efforts in defending London's derivatives traders—mostly subsidiaries of U.S. banks—from EU regulation, let alone taxes, while backing savage austerity programs." (Susan Watkins, "Vanity and Venality," *London Review of Books*, August 29, 2013, p. 20.)

seen as untouchable and non-negotiable collective use-values, such items are now fair game for re-commodification, for buying cheaply only to resell at colossally dearer prices, adaptively reusing them as speculative exchange values, as new terrains for financial and merchant capital, for new accumulation strategies. "Austerians," as the U.S. economist Paul Krugman calls them, prevail in pretty much every country, espousing their quack shock therapies universally. But they lurk in academic communities, too, and the ideology gets peddled by well-known economists as the sole panacea to downturn and economic doldrums, many of whom legitimize austerity policies and provide intellectual bulwarks for government spending cuts, for lay-offs and job slashing, for closing public libraries and hospitals, for land and property giveaways—because it is "healthy" for our economy to do so. To this degree, austerity perversely creates a depression and a crisis that actually serves the interests of the wealthy, of the parasitic 1 percent.[10]

The war against the parasites, in short, is a concerted war against austerians, those in and out of government, those in business, those in the academy, a war of position that means the general will won't

---

10. One of the *cause célèbres* here is the example of Harvard economists Carmen Reinhart and Kenneth Rogoff, whose infamous "Growth in Time of Debt" article, published in the *American Economic Review* (No. 100, 2010), suggests that slump is the right occasion to implement austerity (rather than boom, which would make a lot more sense) and that nations with a public debt burden of greater than 90 percent of their GDP face withered growth and lack of economic vitality. Rather than spend to help people in need, Reinhart and Rogoff brandish data (spurious data as has since been recognized) to authorize cuts and public sector downsizing. The basis of their article, in other words, is totally unfounded. Still, as Krugman says, "the 90% claim was cited as the decisive argument for austerity by figures ranging from Paul Ryan, the former House Budget Committee, to Olli Rehn, the top economic official at the European Commission." "The case for austerity was and is," Krugman concludes, "one that many powerful people want to believe, leading them to seize on anything that looks like a justification . . . As many observers have noted, the turn away from fiscal and monetary stimulus can be interpreted, if you like, as giving creditors priority over workers, increasing the certainty of bondholders that they'll be repaid in full." (Paul Krugman, "How the Case for Austerity has Crumbled," *New York Review of Books*, June 6, 2013, p. 67.)

be deceived, that its sovereignty is the sovereignty of citizens, not the debtocracy of creditors. In the end, or perhaps even at the point of a new beginning, it remains to be seen whether these assorted movements and democratic constellations—the sort I have discussed in this book—have anti-capitalist potentiality, whether they can go the whole ideological and practical hog against austerians and parasites. I sincerely hope they can. Such groups have their own specific characteristics, characteristics culturally and nationally conditioned. Some activism voices dissent against political authoritarianism while other protesters elsewhere denounce economic authoritarianism. Usually the two authoritarianisms go together. Movements share, however, a common enemy: a transnational corporate and financial elite who sets the terms of government policy and of the urban process. At the very least, a democratic awareness has been created, a solidarity between people, spanning different countries, spanning different cities, a solidarity many hadn't known before, one based on shared feeling, shared anger, and shared disgust. People in strange and unforeseen ways have found the means to organize themselves on the ground.

The problem of organization, and of not making demands—as some critics have voiced against Occupy—is thus overstated. People here have shown a tremendous capacity to organize. The issue is more about coordination and objectives. One should have goals, but why demands? Demands imply a certain form of politics of recognition. Demands mean asking for something from somebody. Sure, goals, sure objectives, goals and objectives that maybe do need spelling out from time to time, certainly in the aftermath of any insurrection. But demands? Demands mean you're asking for something, you're asking an interlocutor that you want to be recognized as wanting something. That's a politics of conciliation; that's not at all what should be done. In any event, almost everywhere demands are quite clear, clear about what we don't want, clear that we want something else, something that still needs to be worked out, worked through.

Worked through how? It's impossible to know in advance, without a crystal ball. What we do know is how political struggle and social transformation are very odd things. Sometimes you win, sometimes you lose. Sometimes even when you thought you'd won, it turns out you lost. Sometimes when you lose, you might actually win at a future point. Maybe there are two kinds of political constellation, two kinds of transformative encounters between people, united against those in power: *morphing encounters* and *punctuating encounters*. What unfolds in the former instance is an insurrection, some form of revolt, a collective revolt, of people en masse, in the street, in the public square, people demonstrating, activity frequently violent, leading to a certain transformation of the social relations that existed the day before. And yet, it may transpire that that hasn't really changed anything significant.

Afterwards, you get new form of government, a new bunch of ruling folk who enter office, who wear different clothes, who look different, but who actually go about doing the exact same thing—or nearly the exact same thing. That's probably a little bit like what's gone on in Egypt, and that's what we'd call a "morphing encounter": things just morph into something else; reformism occurs. The second kind of transformation, though, is a "punctuating encounter": the social fabric really does rip apart and nothing's ever going to go back to what it was. 1989 was a punctuating encounter; the French Revolution was a punctuating encounter. Things fundamentally change and change is fundamental. There's a rift; there's a rending of the fabric, of the social fabric, of the political fabric, of the economic fabric—and likely of the urban fabric. The day after, things are never ever going to return to what they once were.

Ironically, if you look at the history of revolutionary movements, what anybody, any historian of revolt will tell you is that often it's incredible how things happen. Historians of the French Revolution confirm how quickly, and how relatively easily, an ostensibly formidable administrative and political-economic system dissipated almost overnight. That's the hopeful side of stuff. The negative side is that all revolts, all social transformations you believe may have won one day can in fact transpire as Pyrrhic victories the day after, or the day after that. You realize that actually the social movement has transformed into something else, that it isn't exactly what you'd expected, even though it's a punctuating encounter in itself; something's happened which isn't what you intended. And there's no way anybody can know this to begin with, prior to engaging in struggle, no secret or double agent, no great escaper or great refuser. You just have to deal with it and see what happens, use foresight and insight, experience and ingenuity, activity and acumen, even as you acknowledge that there's no recipe book, no simple magic formula.

The magic formula I spoke about in *Magical Marxism*[11] is nothing less than the complexity of peoples' imagination, that hopeful and contingent capacity to imagine something else, which we do all the time. It may be trivial; it may not imagine great social formations or systems of government or entire new forms of life. Yet we do imagine nonetheless. We imagine that we're going to be somewhere else tomorrow or next week, that we're going to build something new, going to do something that didn't exist two days ago, or yesterday. That's imagination, that's our capacity to act upon imagination, the magic people possess, making us different from other animals. We can consciously construct things in our imagination before we build them in reality. That's our collective promise, of what we can do programmatically and prospectively. We've done this from time immemorial. Humans destroy all the time, have an inbuilt predilection to wreak havoc on each other. But we also build amazing structures and strange things happen in the meanwhile, and in the aftermath of the meanwhile. Before all else, that's why I'm an optimist and *The New Urban Question* an optimistic book.

11. Andy Merrifield, *Magical Marxism: Subversive Politics and the Imagination*, Pluto Press, London, 2011.

Index